WELCOME TO THE FAMILY

An Introduction to Evangelical Christianity

WILLIAM W. WELLS

INTER-VARSITY PRESS
DOWNERS GROVE
ILLINOIS 60515

InterVarsity Press is the book-publishing division of
Inter-Varsity Christian Fellowship, a student movement active
on campus at hundreds of universities, colleges and
schools of nursing. For information about local and regional
activities, write IVCF, 233 Langdon St., Madison, WI 53703.

Distributed in Canada through InterVarsity Press,
1875 Leslie St., Unit 10, Don Mills, Ontario M3B 2M5, Canada.

All Scripture quotations are from the Revised Standard Version
of the Bible, copyrighted 1946, 1952 © 1971, 1973,
unless otherwise indicated.

ISBN 0-87784-624-3
Library of Congress Catalog Card Number: 78-70807

Printed in the United States of America

To Jane,
who encouraged me
to write

Acknowledgments

Most of this book was written during the 1976-77 academic year while I was on sabbatical leave from the University of Hawaii. I hereby acknowledge my debt to the university for freeing me from classroom responsibilities so that I could work on the project. Some of that year was spent at Fuller Theological Seminary; I would like to express my thanks to Jack Rogers and Ray Anderson for their encouragement and help at an early stage of writing.

Nate Smith, Dick Weikle and Ken Wyneken read the manuscript after it was completed and made helpful suggestions, and Donald Tinder's comments on the opening chapters were quite beneficial. Nigel Biggar, a teaching assistant at Regent College, helped in the preparation of the index, and Oliver Trimiew assisted with the section on the black church in America. In particular, I would like to thank Mike Hayes (the Inter-Varsity Christian Fellowship area director for Hawaii) for bringing my manuscript to the attention of InterVarsity Press and for commenting extensively on the text.

The title of the book is borrowed with permission from the title of a record by Paul Sandberg, a good friend. (Welcome to the Family, Manna Records, MS 2030).

My wife, Jane, read and commented on several successive drafts of the book. If the results are readable, it is in large measure her contribution. These few words in print do not begin to convey my appreciation.

FAMILY
TIES:
INTRODUCTION

1

Becoming a Christian is a lot like getting married. You get a family in the bargain. The wedding may leave you with blurred memories of new faces. But gradually the faces become familiar, and you begin to develop a bond with some of the relatives.

The evangelical family is like that. When you first commit your life to Christ, you might feel pretty much alone. But then you discover that you have become a member of a whole family of people who are also committed to Christ.

Jesus taught his disciples to pray by saying, "Our Father. . . ." (Mt. 6:9). When we receive Christ as our Savior, we become the "children of God" (Jn. 1:12). If God is our Father and we are his children, then all other believers are our brothers and sisters. Jesus said that "whoever does the will of my Father in heaven is my brother, and sister, and mother" (Mt. 12:50).

The purpose of this book is to introduce you to the genealogy of your faith. You and I are branches on a family tree. We need to get to know something about the other branches. The evangelical faith has some surprising roots, and there are some very interesting family members. You may be amazed at the diversity of the family, but I hope that looking at the differences between believers will help you to see the unity more clearly. I think you will also be gratified to know how deep your roots go. They reach back many centuries and out to many lands.

If we are going to examine the essential elements of evangelical Christianity, we need to have a good working definition. Evangelicalism is a significant part—but only a part—of what is commonly called Christianity. It is not a denomination (like the Baptists, Lutherans or Presbyterians); it is, rather, a perspective on the Christian faith that is held by many people from many different denominations. I personally consider it, with all its weaknesses, to be closest to the normative Christianity of the New Testament.

All Christians confess their faith by means of doctrines such as the Trinity (the affirmation that there is one God who has existed from all eternity in three persons: Father, Son and Holy Spirit), the Incarnation (the affirmation that God became man in Jesus Christ), and the atonement (the affirmation that the death of Christ dealt with sin and thus enables each person to return to God). When I use the word *evangelical,* therefore, I have three more specific characteristics in mind:

1. *Evangelicals believe in the unique divine inspiration, entire trustworthiness and authority of the Bible.* This affirmation separates evangelicals theologically from Catholic Christians who hold that authority also lies with the traditions and the teaching office of the Church. Furthermore, this doctrine separates evangelicals from religious groups which claim to possess extrabiblical revelations, such as the *Book of Mormon* or the *Divine Principle* of Sun Myung Moon. Finally, this doctrine separates evangelicals theologically from any form of liberal Protestantism which denies the unique status of the Bible and thus holds it to be one revelation among many.

2. *Evangelicals believe and personally appropriate by faith alone*

God's promise that he will forgive, redeem, justify and accept them into a personal relationship with himself on the basis of the life, death and resurrection of his only Son, Jesus Christ. This assertion separates evangelicals theologically from any group which holds that the sacraments of the church bring salvation apart from serious personal commitment to Jesus Christ.

3. *Evangelicals commit themselves to the pursuit of a holy life and to the disciplines seen as necessary for Christian growth, including Bible study, prayer, fellowship with other Christians and evangelism.* This final affirmation separates evangelicals from nominal Christianity; that is, from a Christianity which gives mere lip service to the disciplines of the faith or which neglects to encourage wholehearted commitment. The word *evangelism* here distinguishes evangelicals from any form of Protestant liberalism which holds Jesus to be one way to God among many ways and which consequently neglects propagating the gospel among people of other faiths.

These three aspects of the evangelical faith correspond roughly to the three parts of this book.

This is not to say that evangelicals agree about everything. Take matters of behavior, for example. The people who brought me into the faith taught me that drinking and smoking are not acceptable habits for Christians. Yet I soon learned that there were many evangelicals who did not share their convictions. Once I attended a "work day" at a church away from home. When lunchtime came around, I was astonished to see several members of the congregation light up cigarettes. And I was even more surprised when the minister came in carrying a six-pack of beer! Some of their values were different from what I had been taught, but these people considered themselves evangelical, as did the folks back home.

Lifestyles also differ widely between Christians—sometimes in the very same congregation. One friend of mine argues that Christians should not encumber themselves with material goods. This friend drives an old, beat-up car to church and wears hand-me-down clothing. Another member of the same congregation drives a large, luxury car and lives in a spacious, modern home. He uses his assets to serve others. Both of these people love God and wish to glorify him; yet their lifestyles are drastically different.

Worship never seems to be the same from one group to the next either. In one city I visited there were two very different churches within a block of each other. One church was in a beautiful, well-preserved old building. The congregation treasured the history of the building as well as the history of their form of worship. They recited an ancient creed each Sunday and used a traditional liturgy. The church down the block was entirely different. The stucco exterior was cracked, and the whole building needed paint. Over the years these repairs were not made, because the congregation considered the building an extraneous bit of architecture. The important thing to them was the worship that went on inside. They could just as easily have rented a hall for their services. Comfort was not important to them, because they were there to praise God and to learn from his Word.

Evangelicals agree about the inspiration and authority of the Bible, yet they often disagree about how to interpret the text. During high school, I remember hearing discussions about the spiritual significance of the Old Testament passages describing the construction of the tabernacle (a portable place of worship used by the Israelites at one time in their history). The people in my old church used a method of interpretation called typology to derive spiritual truths from these seemingly irrelevant verses. Since that time, I have heard this method of interpretation criticized by other evangelical Christians. Yet I am sure that the Christians in my church considered typology a very useful and perfectly acceptable method.

Evangelicals, it seems, disagree about quite a few things—politics, economics, personal and aesthetic values, biblical interpretation, behavioral standards and even some moral issues. In fact, evangelicals disagree over almost everything. But I said *almost*. I am convinced that this diversity hides a deeper, shared commitment to a core of religious values. This core binds together all sorts of individuals and institutions and unites them into one family.

In the chapters that follow we will examine some of the differences among evangelicals in the hope that you will be able to see some family resemblances through the disparity.

In part one I explore questions about the Bible. Why do we consider it authoritative? Which translation is best? What is the difference between Protestant and Catholic Bibles? Will the average person find the Bible difficult to understand? What ideas tie the Old and New Testaments together?

In part two I try to explain how and why evangelical Protestantism came into existence. Evangelicals speak about their faith in ways which reflect their historical background. This section tries to answer some basic questions about the origins of that evangelical perspective.

Part three surveys various aspects of the evangelical lifestyle. This includes short discussions of the importance of prayer, evangelism, social action and church attendance. Many of these disciplines are considered earmarks of contemporary evangelical faith.

As you read, please remember that this book is an introduction to your Christian family. It is not intended to be a detailed, scholarly treatment. There are no footnotes and I do not interact critically with all the issues that come up. My purpose is not to solve the disagreements, but to point out the areas of agreement.

You may want to skip certain sections of the book. I have written as though the book were being read by someone with very little background in Christianity. So if you grew up in an evangelical church, you may already be familiar with some of this material. So skip to the parts that interest you and use them to fill in the gaps in your background.

Finally, you will notice that I have included bibliographies at the end of each chapter. These include books which are relevant to the topics discussed. Most of the books are available in your local Christian bookstore, although some will have to be obtained from a library. In general, the recommended books are not too technical, and a brief description of each is included. I hope that your reading in this book will whet your appetite to read more about your faith.

THE BIBLE: GOD'S WORD TO US

PART I

OUR BOOK:
OPENING THE
BIBLE

2

Shortly after I began to study theology in seminary, I became convinced that God had made a real mistake. He had not provided even one completely systematic book within the Bible. My work, I felt, would have been a good deal easier if he had done so.

In retrospect, I see that the problem was mine. Mentally, I am a Greek. I prefer philosophy to poetry. I like thought which is systematic. I enjoy reading books which develop an idea logically. God, apparently, is not Greek. But even after I had made that discovery, I still did not comprehend the Bible.

I tried another approach. I began to look at the Bible as history. Many students of the Bible have in fact taken it to be just that. But while the Bible records much that is historically true, most biblical books are clearly not history at all. And even those books which appear (at least at first glance) to be straightforward history are likely to disappoint most formal historians.

The accounts which are contained in these "historical" books make no effort to comment on the culture or politics of the period beyond what is needed to make a particular point about God. What then is the Bible, if it is neither a book of systematic theology nor a comprehensive historical treatise?

Most basically the Bible is a diverse collection of writings which, when taken together, recount and interpret the acts of God in history through which he is reconciling all people to himself. In one sense it is history. It records the history of the relationship of God to the human race. In another sense, it is theology because it provides a theological interpretation of history. Above all else, the Bible is God's Word to all people, a description of God's effort to re-establish a relationship with each person.

Christians refer to it as *God's Word* because they believe it was inspired by God himself. But its divine origin should not obscure the fact that it is simultaneously a thoroughly human book. In his divine freedom God chose to speak to humanity through human authors. Although neither aspect ever appears in isolation, an introduction to the Bible must deal with them separately. I will look first at the Bible as the Word of God, the book which has the authority to speak for God himself. Then I will turn to the literary features of the Bible where the human element becomes more apparent. The discussion will include the Bible's basic structure, how it came into being, how its authenticity gained recognition, and how it has been preserved for us today.

Revealed and Inspired
All Christians recognize that God has spoken in our history and that his speech has some claims on our attention. But Christians have differed—sometimes violently—about where and how to listen to God. Christians who call themselves evangelical believe that God speaks today through his written Word, the Bible. They insist that the Bible must stand as the *sole* norm in all matters of faith and practice. By this confession evangelicals set

themselves in opposition to theological positions taken within other parts of the church.

Evangelicals have intense convictions concerning the importance of the Bible. The very intensity of these convictions sometimes perplexes nonevangelicals. Perhaps the best way to explain these feelings is to contrast the evangelical position to the positions taken by other Christians. We can begin by looking at the Catholic Church.

The Roman Catholic Church claims to possess the tradition of the apostles and to be the only authentic guardian of it. Catholic doctrine clearly asserts the divine origin and authority of the Bible, but claims that the Bible is only a part of that body of tradition. Only the Church, therefore, which possesses the whole of that tradition, is capable of determining the authentic interpretation of the Bible.

When the Reformation began in 1517, the Reformers (the leaders of this movement to change the Church) responded to this claim by saying that the Bible, and it alone, has the right to determine the nature of the Christian faith. The Bible, according to the Reformers, authenticates itself; its authority does not depend on the Church. Furthermore, the Bible is clear enough to be understood by individual believers; an authoritative interpretation by the Church is unnecessary. By God's own choice, the Word of revelation became a written Word. And this written Word has through the centuries stood in judgment over all human institutions, including religious ones.

In the centuries after the Reformation, some who had been reared within the Protestant tradition began to question this theological stance. The eighteenth-century deists, for example, refused to accept any belief which was not confirmed by human reason. This position in effect grants reason the right to stand in judgment over the Bible. In the nineteenth century liberal Protestants began to judge the ethical precepts in the Bible on the basis of their own moral values. Conscience was thereby proclaimed the norm in matters of practice. In both cases individuals determined for themselves what was acceptable in the

Bible. They stood, in effect, in judgment over the Bible.

Evangelical Protestants since the Reformation have consistently, and indeed insistently, affirmed the right of the Bible to stand in judgment over the church, human reason and conscience. Two terms in particular provide the theological foundation of the evangelical doctrine of the Word of God.

Revelation, the first of these two terms, means "disclosure." So revelation in its theological sense means "God's self-disclosure to man." A distinction is often made between "natural" and "special" revelation. God's "natural" revelation, his self-revelation through the created world, is visible today. But it is not adequate to bring us to salvation because our sin stifles our natural awareness of God's reality. Indeed, according to Paul's letter to the Romans, the act of suppressing the awareness of God and his demands warps our reason and conscience. If all people are thus blinded to some degree, then neither reason nor conscience can be trusted to function in a reliable way. They certainly cannot function as judges of God's Word.

In recognition of the human predicament, God chose at the very beginning to reveal himself in a more direct way. God has entered our world throughout the course of history. He has come to us within time and space. In these "special" revelations, God both acted and spoke to redeem the human race from its own self-imposed evil. For example, the book of Exodus, the second book of the Bible, records the fact that God liberated the people of Israel from slavery in Egypt. But that was not all. The book also records that God spoke to these people through his prophet Moses in order to interpret for them what he had done. God declared through Moses that he had liberated them physically in order to become their God.

Inspiration is the second major theological term. The word speaks of the action of God's Holy Spirit which enabled his chosen prophets and apostles to communicate exactly what he intended. In writing, these inspired men of God used their own ordinary languages and the literary forms that were typical of their day. Yet within this very human activity, God himself was at work. God chose to convey his Word through their words. Evangelicals confess that the result of this divine/human activity is truly the inspired Word of God.

When light shines through a prism, it is refracted into a spectrum. It is most certainly not flawed by the prism. In fact, the prism makes the light even more beautiful to us because without it our limited human eyes are unable to perceive the colors. But while the prism does not mar the light, it does alter its form. In a similar way, when the Word of God comes to us through individual human authors, the humanity of the instrument which God chose can be seen in the product. We can actually see different human personalities as we look at various books of the Bible. The Greek style and vocabulary of the apostle John is simple when compared with that of the gospel writer Luke; the difference can be seen even in the English. Yet both men were chosen by God to write his Word.

In a broader sense all human culture helped to shape the Word of God. The wisdom tradition, a literary style which was common in the ancient Near East for more than a thousand years prior to the time of Jesus, gives form and beauty to God's Word in Proverbs. And the Gospels reflect their specific historical background on virtually every page. When we listen as Jesus differs with the Herodians and the Sadducees, we hear God's Word as it was refracted by the first-century culture of Palestine. Through this variety we hear the Word of God.

At times a third term, *illumination,* is added to revelation and inspiration. This term refers to the work of the Holy Spirit in enabling readers to understand God's Word and empowering them to act on it. This concept will be discussed further in chapters three and eleven.

In sum, sin has warped our human reason and conscience. We in turn corrupt all of our human institutions, including the church. Consequently all people must stand under the judgment of God's Word. It demands our obedience, whether as individuals or as the church, and it alone stands as the rightful authority in all matters of faith and practice. This position is of importance to evangelicals today, just as it was important to the Protestant Reformers over four hundred years ago.

An Old Covenant and a New

Turning now from the authority of the Bible to the actual text, we note its most basic structural element: it is divided into an Old Testament and a New Testament. Unfortunately the term *testament*, which occurs in both of these titles, is a misleading translation of a common Hebrew word. The English word *testament* usually refers to a legal will. But the Hebrew word *berith* which is translated as *testament* has nothing to do with legal wills. It is rather a relational term which should be translated as *covenant*. In the Old Testament a covenant is always an agreement between two parties. Most frequently it is an agreement which defines the relationship between God and his people.

God's offer to enter into this covenant relationship is one of the major themes of both the Old and the New Testaments. The offer, which recurs so frequently it would be monotonous if it were not so wonderful, never rests on what any person has done. Rather, it rests on the love of God for all people. Whenever the offer is accepted, a covenant relationship is created which binds God and his people together. God promises to bless his people who in turn promise to serve and obey him. Both parties are obligated to act in ways which maintain the covenant relationship.

The Old Testament, as a record of the beginning and early growth of God's covenant relationship with his people, describes several specific covenant occasions, such as Noah's flood or the giving of the law to Moses. On each occasion, God helped his people to transcend their previous understanding of the covenant and of their obligation to him. Thus God acted through the centuries to deepen and enrich his people's perception of the nature of their special relationship. By the time of the prophet Jeremiah (31:31-34) we see hints of a new covenant which would transform our inner being, not merely our external behavior.

A new covenant was, in fact, created through the work of

Jesus Christ. As a covenant written on the heart, this new covenant brought to fulfillment the whole of Old Testament history. Since that time the new covenant has been available to all
people. All those who have responded to the offer of a covenant
relationship with God have received the Holy Spirit which was
promised. The old covenant was not abrogated. Rather, it finds
its culmination in the new covenant.

How We Got the Bible
From what has been said so far, it should be clear that the Bible
as a physical record came into being over an extended period of
time. As soon as we ask "How long?" we have ceased to study the
Bible solely as God's written revelation and have begun to view
the text itself as an object of historical investigation. This kind
of investigation is known as "higher criticism," and the particular question just raised is only one of many which would normally be raised within the field. Other relevant questions might
be, Where and when did the writers and their readers live? What
events may have motivated them? What source material, if any,
did the writers employ?

Tradition says that the Old Testament was begun by Moses
about 1440 B.C. (some say 1280 B.C.) and was finished around
400 B.C. Some scholars have argued that, while some of the material contained within the so-called five books of Moses (Genesis
through Deuteronomy) may stem from an early period, the actual text of these books could not have been assembled until 950
B.C. (and perhaps as late as 550 B.C.). These same scholars
would also tend to date the final books of the Old Testament
somewhat later, perhaps as late as 150 B.C. The differences in
the conclusions of various scholars can sometimes be traced to
the significantly different assumptions with which they began.

While it took roughly a millennium for the Old Testament to
be composed, the New Testament books were written in less
than a hundred years. Scholars of all stripes date the first letters
of Paul at about A.D. 48. The last books to be written were completed somewhere between A.D. 70 and 120. Most evangelical

scholars would hold that the Bible was written over a period of about fifteen hundred years, from about 1440 B.C. (or 1280 B.C.) to about A.D. 100.

As an anthology the Bible would, of course, have multiple authorship. No one knows, as a matter of fact, who wrote some of the individual books, but an estimate of thirty-five to forty authors would not be far out of line. Most of the writers were Jewish, but they composed their works in such diverse places as Palestine, Babylon, Asia Minor, Greece and Rome. The purposes which motivated this extraordinarily diverse group of authors were undoubtedly as different as they were themselves.

I have spoken so far of the Old Testament and the New Testament as if these terms represented two clearly defined groups of books. In general of course they do. But even today questions regarding the precise limits of the Old Testament disturb the church. And new Christians are sometimes quite surprised to learn of books not included in the New Testament which were read as Scripture by some early Christians. These facts naturally provoke questions such as, Who decided which books should be included in the Bible? How did they decide and could the decision be changed? Could we, for example, add a new book to the Bible or omit one which has traditionally been included? Why do Catholics include material in their Bibles which is not included by many Protestants? Each of these questions concerns itself with one basic problem—that of establishing the *canon* of the Bible.

The origins of the term *canon* are obscure, but we know how the early church used the term. In that context it referred to the list of books which were considered to be authoritative. These books could be used as the rule or standard to measure correct doctrine. The church actually has two canons, the Old Testament, which it inherited from the Jews, and the New Testament, which was written by members of the church. So our questions about the biblical canon must be raised for each of the Testaments in turn.

The authority of the Old Testament came to be recognized in

three phases. First, the *Law* was acknowledged to be from God. Later the writings of numerous Jewish historians and prophets were conjoined as the *Prophets*. This collection was added to the Law as a second distinct body of literature. Finally, during the intertestamental period (the three or four centuries just prior to the birth of Jesus), a somewhat more diversified group of literary works known as the *Writings* gradually obtained canonical status as well. So by the beginning of the first century, the Hebrew Old Testament contained three relatively distinct blocks of literature: the Law, the Prophets and the Writings. There were other pieces of literature written by Jews during and shortly after the intertestamental period, but the rabbis of Palestine concluded, sometime shortly after the destruction of Jerusalem in A.D. 70, that the canon of the Old Testament was closed. It contained exactly thirty-nine books.

The simplicity of the situation was disturbed, however, by events occurring among the Jews who had fled to Egypt centuries before. Out of concern for the generations which no longer spoke Hebrew, these Alexandrian Jews had translated the Hebrew Old Testament into Greek, thus creating the Septuagint translation. In so doing, they unwittingly created a problem for the church because their Greek translation contained books which do not appear in the Hebrew Bible. These additional books, called the "Apocrypha" by Protestants, have been the cause of much discussion, debate and even dissension. The Septuagint circulated widely during the first century, even within Palestine where Aramaic was the local language. Since the New Testament authors wrote in Greek, they tended to use this particular version when they quoted from the Old Testament. They alluded to Apocryphal books only rarely, however, and never as if the books had canonical authority.

Since most of the early Christians spoke and wrote most comfortably in Greek, they also used the Septuagint for worship and study. Unlike Christ and the apostles, however, they did not limit themselves to the thirty-nine books recognized by Palestinian Jews. In fact, some church leaders read and quoted from the Apocryphal books as if they were canonical. Others refused to acknowledge them as authoritative. (Jerome, for instance, refused to include the Apocryphal books in the Vulgate, his Latin translation of the Bible.) By the fifth century, however, those who favored the inclusion of the Apocryphal books had prevailed.

During the Reformation, questions concerning the authority of the Apocrypha were again raised. The Protestant Reformers decided to return to the Hebrew canon in imitation of Christ and the apostles. The Catholic Church reaffirmed its traditional allegiance to the larger Greek canon at the Council of Trent. Consequently, since that time editions of the Bible approved by the Catholic Church contain the Apocrypha, while Protestant Bibles normally omit it. The common impression that Protestant and Catholic Bibles are basically different is ungrounded. There is a dispute, but only about whether or not to grant canonicity to the Apocrypha.

The process by which the New Testament attained canonicity is another story altogether. Paul's collected letters began to circulate as a unit among the churches by the end of the first century. There is also evidence that a fourfold Gospel was in use by the middle of the second century. In addition, individual churches read and treasured a variety of gospels and letters. Some were undoubtedly apostolic in origin. Others made questionable claims of apostolic authorship. And still others were known to have been written by recognized, second generation Christian leaders. But since the concept of an inspired New Testament had not yet emerged, no one thought to differentiate canonical from noncanonical Christian literature. Individuals and churches might have favorites, of course, but there was as yet no consensus.

About A.D. 140 an event occurred which forced the church to begin to define the limits of the New Testament canon. A Roman Christian named Marcion tried to convince the church that it should deny its Jewish roots entirely. In order to encourage this process, Marcion produced his own version of a suitable canon of the Bible. He excluded all of the Old Testament, as well as most of the writings which were then circulating in the church. He concluded that only an edited version of Paul's letters and part of Luke's Gospel should have authority within the church.

Marcion's heresy contributed to the development of the church even though the church at Rome officially denounced him in A.D. 144. He succeeded in forcing the church to begin to define the canon, a process which occupied the church's attention for about the next two hundred years. In the end the church recognized twenty-seven books which officially constituted a New Testament. By the same token it declared that the rest of the literature which had been circulating among the churches had value only as devotional aids or as theological reflections. And finally, the church reaffirmed the continuing value of the Old Testament. Henceforth, the twenty-seven books consciously recognized as a New Testament would, together with the Old Testament, constitute the Bible.

The historical process we have just examined shows how completely God's Word is involved in human history. Out of conflicting historical pressures, a book emerged which Christians take to be the Word of God. But that is only half the story. Christians believe that God was invisibly active in the midst of the observable events, bringing to pass what he had willed. The church asked whether a particular book was written by an apostle or a prophet and thereby demonstrated that it valued certain external marks of authority. But in the end the decisive question was: Does it speak with the authority of God? The church did not create the Bible or grant it authority. On the contrary, the church recognized and listened to the voice of her Lord speaking in and through certain pieces of literature. These she recognized as Scripture and so formed a fixed canon for her own use.

In sum, decisions made by the church five hundred or even fifteen hundred years ago continue to influence the corporate life of even the smallest local congregation in very concrete ways. The canon of books approved by the Catholic Church during

the medieval period is readily available in a variety of translations at most local bookstores. The same is true of the canon approved by the Protestant Reformers. But it is more difficult to
locate a copy of the noncanonical book Shepherd of Hermas,
for example, even though the book was widely read in the early
church. The universal church has effectively closed the debate
on the contents of the biblical canon, except perhaps in academic circles. This decision is one of the factors which governs
the form of worship used by every individual congregation.

More and More Translations
Because of the dissension caused by Marcion and others like
him, the church was forced to establish a fixed canon for herself.
In contrast, the translation of the Bible has rarely been controlled by the church in this formal way. Protestants in particular
have been tolerant of diversity in this area. In fact Protestants
began to translate the Bible into languages other than Latin at
the very outset of the Reformation. Martin Luther, for example,
had begun his German translation by 1521, and English translations were circulating widely only 15 years later. However, the
early translation which received the widest acceptance in the
English-speaking world was the King James Version. This translation was authorized by the King of England and appeared in
1611. Even today it remains in wide use along with excellent
twentieth-century translations.

In recent years the very wealth of translations available to
English-speaking Protestants has become somewhat of a problem. The variety disturbs many Christians, and it is especially
confusing for those new to the faith. Consequently, it is helpful
to understand why there are so many translations of the Bible,
what differentiates them from one another, and how to select
a translation of the Bible for personal use.

Until about 1450 when printing was first invented, copies of
the Bible had to be handwritten. Thus prior to that time the
Bible could have been altered or corrupted by the slip of a pen.
God in his providence might have preserved the text of the Bible

unchanged throughout the ages, but he did not. On the contrary the variant readings which appear in the ancient manuscripts of the Bible suggest that alteration of the text began almost at once.

Textual criticism—a specialized branch of biblical studies—is the effort to reconstruct the original text out of these variant readings. During the last century, biblical scholars have made tremendous advances in this field. As a result of their labors, a vast number of manuscripts have been edited and become available. The principles for dealing with the alternative readings contained in the manuscripts have been honed into a science. And most important of all, the Hebrew and Greek texts which have become available to biblical translators closely approximate the original. This very process of reconstructing the original text, however, calls for subjective judgments. So disagreements among the textual critics concerning precise wordings are inevitable. And these differences lead to differences in translation. Here, then, is the first major reason for the large number of recent translations: each one is based on a slightly different reconstruction of the original Greek and Hebrew texts.

The ongoing debate among translators regarding the proper approach to their task provides a second reason. Some translators argue that translations should follow the word order of the original language as closely as possible in order to be faithful to the author's intent. The American Standard Version (1901), an excellent older example of this approach, has been widely used by those who wished to study the English text in detail in order to grasp the precise meaning of the original. Its literal approach has commended it to several generations of seminary students as an aid to studying the Hebrew and Greek texts. The New American Standard Bible (1963), a recent revision of this earlier version, has been accepted by the public for the same reasons. Critics of this approach are quick to point out, however, that translations based on this word-for-word approach may be misleading because any two languages differ in syntax. Furthermore, the results tend to be rather wooden in style.

People at the opposite end of the spectrum argue that the essence of any text is its meaning, and that these meanings should be put into good idiomatic English by a paraphrase. The tremendous popularity of the Living Bible (1971) in the United States indicates that the public appreciates a Bible whose language has a familiar ring. Critics of the Living Bible, on the other hand, contend that it is not just a paraphrase at all. It is rather a commentary in disguise. They insist that it is understandable precisely because the difficulties found in the original text have been minimized.

Most scholars, however, reject these extremes and strive instead for a balance between idiomatic English on the one hand and precise fidelity to the word order of the original text on the other. The Revised Standard Version (1952), the Jerusalem Bible (1966), the New English Bible (1970), the Good News Bible (1976) and the New International Version (1978) are excellent, recently published examples of this mediating approach.

A third reason for divergent translations is simply the fact that our language is constantly changing. Consequently, there will always be the tension between traditional literary forms and newer modes of expression.

It is not likely that agreement will ever be reached regarding the proper rendering of any particular biblical passage, much less of the Bible as a whole. New translations will continue to appear in print just as they always have in the past.

How should evangelicals respond to this wave of new versions of the Bible? First of all, we should be grateful. God has raised up gifted people to nourish the body of Christ by their gifts in the field of biblical studies, in general, and in the task of translation, in particular. But still, how do you make good use of this new wealth of translations?

Here I would like to venture some cautious suggestions for the newcomer to the faith. First of all, choose one of the "mediating" translations—one which is neither a paraphrase nor an extremely literal rendition of the text. It will probably be most useful on the whole. Second, when studying a particular passage in depth, compare two or more of these translations. This process will often sharpen the meaning of that particular passage. Finally, have confidence in God. The newer translations disagree in places, but none of these disagreements will be decisive for your faith. God has been using translations which are only more or less accurate throughout the history of the church. He is not limited by errors in translation. So read, mark, study and inwardly digest the Bible in confidence. God will always use his Word.

Further Reading

Bruce, F. F. *The Books and the Parchments.* Old Tappan, N.J.: Revell, 1963. An informative discussion of the transmission of the Bible from ancient times to the present.

Bruce, F. F. *The English Bible: A History of Translations.* New York: Oxford Univ. Press, 1970. A standard work in the field by a well-known British evangelical.

Harris, R. Laird. *The Inspiration and Canonicity of the Bible.* Grand Rapids: Zondervan, 1969. Takes an evangelical approach to both subjects.

Packer, J. I. *Fundamentalism and the Word of God: Some Evangelical Principles.* Grand Rapids: Eerdmans, 1958. A short, but thorough exposition of the evangelical approach to biblical inspiration.

Wenham, John W. *Christ and the Bible.* Downers Grove, Ill.: InterVarsity Press, 1972. A short study of the way Christ viewed the Old Testament. The author argues that Christians should view the Bible as Jesus did.

HOW TO READ
THE BIBLE:
INTERPRETING THE WORD

3

When I first became a Christian, I was led to believe that good Christians ought to read the Bible, but no one ever explained to me (at least not clearly) why this was so. Apparently this mandate was thought to be so obvious that nothing needed to be said.

In retrospect I am absolutely convinced that my pastors and teachers were right in encouraging me to read the Bible. Yet in talking with friends I have become aware of two reasons why people do not read it. First, they are not convinced that it is worth the effort. Second, they are not convinced that the average reader can understand the book. So before we move on to the main point of the chapter—how to read the Bible—let's look at these two preliminary issues.

Why study the Bible? Almost all students are told at some stage in their education that "reading Shakespeare is good for you." Those who say so must find Shakespeare helpful in their own lives; in any case, they seem to enjoy the experience. But the fact is that a lot of people do not enjoy Shakespeare and are not enriched by an encounter with his work. Apparently knowing

Shakespeare is not essential to maturity even though some people find it helpful.

Is it possible that the same holds true for the Bible? Clearly, the answer is, No. In fact the question is founded on a basic misunderstanding. To argue that knowledge of the Bible is a luxury on a par with knowledge of Shakespeare is to miss a fundamental distinction. The Bible is not just a piece of good literature. There is an infinite difference between poetic inspiration and the inspiration of the Bible by the Holy Spirit. God himself chose to speak to us. That fact alone should provide a presumption in favor of reading the Bible, but there is a second reason too.

We enter the Christian life by faith and, as Paul teaches, faith comes by hearing the Word of God. Faith does not, however, end at the moment of salvation. On the contrary, we live the whole of our Christian life by faith. It follows that ongoing contact with the Word of God is essential for Christian growth. As the meaning and personal significance of the Word are understood, the Holy Spirit uses that understanding to convict us of sin and nurture our growth in Christ. He teaches us to live by faith through our contact with the Word. Evangelical Christians agree on this. That is why we read and study the Bible.

Can the average reader understand the Bible? Sometimes Christians are determined to read the Bible, but run into problems when they do. Everyone seems to get a different meaning from it. And if that is the case, then what right does any one person have to assume that his or her interpretation is correct? The conflicting interpretations discourage people from even attempting to understand Scripture.

Those who are troubled by this problem acknowledge, at least implicitly, that knowing God's Word is important. But they see no way to attain that knowledge. The effort appears hopeless. It is true that disagreement regarding the meaning of the biblical text is pervasive. But we must face the issue squarely. Either the text is hopelessly obscure and inherently ambiguous—and God is a bungler—or the problem lies with the reader. I choose to believe, as evangelical Protestants have always believed, that the Bible is clear, trustworthy and infallible. It does not fail to accomplish what God intends for it. Therefore, the problem must lie with the reader.

So the question shifts slightly. Why is it that a book which is inherently clear is so frequently misunderstood? The most obvious answer is simply that readers are careless. To say that the Bible is clear is not to say it is simple. Some readers do not expend the energy necessary for understanding. But this only partially answers the question. Some Christians come to the text with a sincere desire to read and understand what God is saying. They try, and yet they still do not understand. The history of the church is full of heretics with good intentions.

Here we come to the nub of the problem and the reason for this chapter. Sometimes people who read the Bible employ faulty methods of interpretation and thereby preclude any possibility of rightly understanding the text. The fundamental problem, as I see it, is the lack of an adequate and clearly understood method of interpretation. Contrary to popular belief, biblical interpreters who use an appropriate method of interpretation achieve a surprising degree of unanimity.

The first section of this chapter introduces several methods of interpretation, all of which have been used and are currently being used within evangelical churches. This historical survey will lay a foundation for constructing an alternative method.

Methods of Biblical Interpretation

Typological interpretation. When the early church broke with Judaism, a variety of theological problems arose almost immediately. One of the thorniest of these concerned the authority of the Old Testament. Was the Old Testament the Word of God for the church or not? The early Christians assumed that it was, but interpreting it from a Christian perspective proved to be a problem. One early response to this particular issue was typological interpretation. According to advocates of this method, some events or ritual practices in the Old Testament are symbolic of truths which are clarified (or even events which occur) in the New Testament. The careful expositor should, therefore, note and explicate such parallels between the two Testaments. The method rests on several assumptions: (1) that there is a fundamental theological unity between the two Testaments; (2) that events recounted in the Old Testament may be historically true and at the same time possess a significance which transcends history; and (3) that many concepts and principles which are spelled out in detail within the New Testament are, as a matter of fact, prefigured or implied within the Old Testament.

The first attempts to use this approach occur within the New Testament itself. The author of Hebrews (in chapter 7) begins one of his typological arguments by reminding his readers of two passages: Genesis 14:17-20, which mentions Melchizedek, the priest of the city of Salem; and Psalms 110:4, which reads, "You are a priest for ever after the order of Melchizedek." The author then begins the exposition. The name Melchizedek means "king of righteousness," and this rather enigmatic character was king of Salem, which means "peace." The Old Testament records neither the names of his parents nor his lineage; and neither the beginning nor the end of his life is mentioned. He is, therefore, a proper *type* (symbol or model) of Christ. The importance of Melchizedek is this: as Abraham returned from battle on one occasion, he paid a tithe of his booty to Melchizedek. This act seems to imply, at least for the author of Hebrews, that Melchizedek is greater than Abraham or any of Abraham's descendants including his descendant Aaron, the first high priest of the Mosaic system. Since Jesus is a priest "after the order of Melchizedek," his priesthood is a greater priesthood than that which was instituted under the Mosaic law. So, the author of Hebrews concludes, it would be foolish to abandon this Greater Priest in order to return to Judaism.

It is important to note that the author of Hebrews does not deny the historicity of Melchizedek. He insists, however, that the Genesis text has a significance which transcends history. The historical person of Melchizedek actually prefigures the

Christ. By using a typological approach to the Old Testament, the author of Hebrews was able to transform the Old Testament into an explicitly Christian book.

Evangelical Christians are presently divided on how to evaluate this kind of interpretation. Since Hebrews is a part of the Bible, its typological sections claim our respect as the Word of God. But some biblical expositors argue that we can use only those types which are explicitly developed for us in the New Testament. To do more, they claim, is to risk becoming arbitrary in our exposition.

Others argue that the book of Hebrews demonstrates that the procedure is legitimate. We know that the truth of God remains constant throughout both Testaments. Therefore, we should expect to find, and indeed we should look for, other types. The argument is plausible; however, some expositors have carried typology to extremes and by so doing have helped to discredit the approach. Even where the method is not taken to extremes, people frequently neglect to see the meaning inherent in a passage because of their eagerness to see it as a type of something else.

Allegorical interpretation. In allegory, foreign elements or ideas are read into the text, thereby assigning it a "deeper" meaning. The original meaning is often ignored or even denied outright. To one who is new to biblical studies, this kind of interpretation might appear initially to be another name for typology, but there are differences. In typology the historical significance and the context of a passage are played down, but they are not denied altogether. In allegory the natural sense of a passage may well be repudiated intentionally.

Augustine's interpretation of the parable of the Good Samaritan (Lk. 10:25-37) is a suitable illustration of this method. The original story is about a man who was mugged on a trip to Jericho. A priest and a Levite passed him by, choosing to ignore the man's obvious needs. Then a Samaritan, belonging to a race despised by most Jews, stopped, rendered assistance and in Jesus' eyes showed true love.

Christ tells this story to a lawyer in answer to the question, Who is my neighbor? But this context is completely ignored by Augustine, and the parable becomes instead the story of Everyman.

Everyman is on a journey toward eternity when he is overtaken by the devil and his demons who try to destroy him. The Old Testament priesthood can no longer offer any assistance. But Christ, the rejected One, rescues Everyman and entrusts his care to the church. Augustine's allegory has two problems. First, all of this theology had to be imported into the text. Second, the question which provoked the parable in the beginning remains unexamined and unanswered. Augustine told a good story, but the point Jesus intended to make was missed.

This approach to interpretation originated among the ancient Greeks in their efforts to reconcile the mythical poetry of Homer and Hesiod with the teaching of the philosophers. When Christians later brought the gospel to the Greeks, they found themselves at a cultural disadvantage as they tried to communicate it. Parts of the Old Testament embarrassed them, just as these difficult sections had embarrassed Philo (an early Jewish philosopher who interpreted the Old Testament allegorically to reconcile it with sophisticated Greek philosophy). How, for example, could there be "days" of creation before the sun and moon were made on the fourth "day"? And were Christians to believe that God had a physical body and experienced human emotion as the Old Testament seemed to imply? The key was found in 2 Corinthians 3:6 where it says, "The written code kills, but the Spirit gives life." In context this passage has nothing to do with methods of interpretation, but it provided an excuse for allegorizing the Old Testament. Within a Greek context this was a respectable solution, but it eventually raised problems of its own.

Advocates of a variety of heretical theologies adopted the allegorical method to "find" their ideas in the Bible. The Gnostics (an early sect which taught that matter was inherently evil and accordingly sought to transcend matter to reach total spirituality) allegorized the New Testament in order to delete the doctrine of the Incarnation, which they found offensive. They thereby alienated themselves from the mainstream of the church. But when questioned, they accused Christians of being inconsistent by limiting the use of the method to the Old Testament. So the church was confronted with a fundamental problem; that is, that there were no obvious checks on what can be "found" in the Bible once allegory is accepted as a legitimate mode of interpretation. Consequently the church was forced to augment the allegorical approach with an authoritative method of biblical interpretation.

Authoritative interpretation. The Gnostics were in error, according to the church, because they injected meanings from their own tradition into the Bible. These meanings contradicted the teachings of the church. Naturally it was asked, Whose traditions should be followed? Toward the end of the second century, Irenaeus argued that the church is the guardian of Scripture. Since the proper interpretation of the text has been passed down within the church, the church's interpretation must be the correct one. Tertullian, another early church leader, argued along similar lines. Since the Scriptures belong legally to the church, only the church has the right to interpret them.

This answer effectively barred Gnostic interpretation of the Bible, but it did not settle matters internally. How should the Scriptures be interpreted by those who stand within the church? Here again, the opinions of Irenaeus and Tertullian are of interest. They agreed that the Bible must be interpreted according to the "rule of faith"; that is, according to the common Christian creed. Several centuries later, Vincent of Lerins specified that the Bible must be interpreted according to the "Catholic faith," which he defined as that which has been believed and taught "everywhere, always, and by everyone." All three were saying in effect that only the church has the authority to interpret the Bible.

Liberal/critical interpretation. In the aftermath of the Renaissance, the bond between philosophy and theology began to weaken. Time and time again, philosophers tried to formulate a picture of the cosmos apart from any dependence upon biblical revelation. One result of this effort was a gradual separation between philosophy and biblical Christianity, a separation which led in time to antagonism between the two fields and eventually to a complete divorce. In the eighteenth century, deists argued that God would not—perhaps could not—intervene in the world. The concepts of miracles and revelation were left over, they claimed, from a more credulous age.

This position, if accepted, leads to the conclusion that the Bible could not possibly be the Word of God. It must be merely another piece of religious literature. If this is so, we have no guarantee that it is true. We must assume that everything in the book is totally conditioned by the historical and cultural context of the writers and that we are free to reject whatever seems unreasonable. Thus the so-called liberal or critical method of interpretation is an attempt to study the Bible apart from the Christian presupposition that it is God's Word. During the nineteenth century, a great number of biblical scholars accepted both this method and its presuppositions.

The problem with this method is obvious to evangelicals today. We believe that God intervenes in history and that the Bible is his Word. Any acceptable method of biblical interpretation must be compatible with these presuppositions. Therefore, although aspects of the critical method of interpretation may be maintained, the underlying presuppositions must not be.

Spirit-led interpretation. Spirit-led interpretation, though called by various names, has reappeared regularly throughout the history of the church. Its advocates assert that only the Holy Spirit, who inspired the Word, can reveal its true meaning to the reader.

A fine line separates *Spirit-led interpretation* from *illumination,* an important theological concept which has always been a part of the Protestant doctrine of Scripture. According to sixteenth-century Protestant Reformers, God originally revealed his Word through the Holy Spirit, but the Word remains cold and distant until the Holy Spirit completes his work. He must illuminate the hearts and minds of readers so that they grasp the personal significance of the text. For example, the Spirit may use a particular text to convict people of sin or to draw them to worship. The Spirit does *not,* however, communicate additional content. Anyone can read and understand what the words say, but only the person who is moved internally by the Holy Spirit hears with the heart. Evangelicals are in agreement on this concept of illumination.

But Spirit-led interpretation goes one important step further. Advocates of this approach insist that the Holy Spirit not only illuminates the hearts of thoughtful readers who use their minds to study God's revealed Word, but he may also speak with readers directly to communicate *new* and hitherto unrevealed content. The concept of illumination asserts that the Spirit utilizes what the readers' minds understand to speak to their spirits. Advocates of Spirit-led interpretation insist that the Spirit speaks directly to the heart, without necessarily utilizing the written text of the Bible. So according to advocates of this position, readers of the Word should listen primarily to the Holy Spirit who speaks within them.

This approach is open to serious objections. It tends to make the text of the Bible superfluous, and it depreciates unnecessarily the value of the intellect in Bible study.

All of the methods of interpretation discussed so far are used within the evangelical community. But most evangelical leaders today advocate so-called natural interpretation. Therefore this method will receive a more thorough explanation.

Observing, Interpreting, Applying: The Natural Method
Some people would refer to this method of interpretation as a literal approach, but I prefer the term *natural.* In reality they are the same. The problem is that sometimes the *literal* approach to the Bible is confused with the *hyperliteral* approach, in spite of repeated efforts to clarify the distinction. A simple example should serve. The Old Testament occasionally refers to the "eye of the Lord." Since literalists are willing to recognize simile and

metaphor in the text, they would interpret the phrase as a reference to God's omniscience. Hyperliteralists would feel compelled to conclude that God has a physical eye. In order to avoid this misunderstanding, some literalists choose to refer to their approach as natural interpretation. Others call it by its complete, but cumbersome title—historical-grammatical-cultural interpretation. All of these tags mean roughly the same thing. The adherents of this position assert that the text means exactly *what the author intended it to mean*. Poetry should be interpreted as poetry, metaphor as metaphor, history as history and so on.

The reason evangelicals prefer the natural approach is quite straightforward. It is the only approach which is consistent with the concept of the Bible expressed in the previous chapter. Evangelical Christians continually return to and reaffirm the notion that God has spoken to us infallibly and authoritatively through the writings of individuals who were expressly chosen for their task. Consequently we are compelled to ask, What did God intend to say through these writers?

Of course, we have no direct access to the intent of God. We have only the words which the Holy Spirit inspired the authors to use. So we must rephrase our question as, What did the biblical authors intend to say? Readers employing natural interpretation are eager to clarify the intention of each particular author by studying the words chosen under the inspiration of the Spirit. Most evangelical teachers use this method of interpretation precisely because of their tremendous respect for God's Word. By the same token, they tend to reject the methods discussed previously because none of them is primarily concerned with the intent of the original author.

Seeing the intent of an author in a text is difficult. There are no two ways about that! But it is a skill that can be learned. The process which enables us to hear in the Bible what God is saying to us today can be summarized in three steps.

Observation. This first step constitutes the basic difference between natural interpretation and the methods discussed in previous sections. Each of the other approaches moves directly to interpretation or to application without first observing with care what the text *actually says*. This point cannot be overemphasized. Observation means disciplining yourself to take the time to examine the actual words and structures of the text. In order to enhance your ability to do that—and as an aid to your patience —ask yourself some of these questions:

1. Who are the people mentioned in the text?
2. Where did this event occur?
3. When did it occur?
4. What do the various terms used in this text mean?
5. What literary form did the author use (poetry, parable, letter, etc.)?
6. How is the passage structured?

The text itself will answer many of these questions. But in some areas you will need help. After all, the biblical writers wrote for people who lived and died some twenty to thirty-five centuries ago. We need to hear with their ears before we can listen with our own. And that will be difficult.

A basic problem faced by readers of the Bible is that each book was written within a particular cultural context, and the writers naturally assumed that their readers would know that context. But because twentieth-century readers do not come from the same environment, they lack the cultural knowledge which the writer presupposed. Hence they may miss the point. Looking at the environment in which the Bible was written should reveal clues for interpreting a particular text.

So as you read, you should be primarily interested in collecting information which is available within the text itself. When you become aware that you lack some important piece of information which would have been available to the original audience, you will have to go outside your Bible to find it. The bibliography at the end of this chapter suggests some books which will help you answer such questions as: What sort of city was Corinth? What was Paul's training and how might it have influenced his writing? What kind of place was Ninevah and why was Jonah so reluctant to go there?

These sorts of questions will help you to notice the particular details within a text which unlock the whole. You cannot possibly know in advance which details will be significant. Consequently, you can hardly avoid discovering details by this process which will prove to be relatively unimportant. Nonetheless, the meanings contained in the text will always rest on some detail or another. After you have looked closely at the words and structures of the text, you are ready and equipped to inquire about its meaning.

Interpretation. Interpretation is the process by which the reader uses the observed data to clarify the ideas of the author. There is cause for confidence at this point. It is unlikely that you will project your own ideas onto the text after you have disciplined yourself to observe it. On the contrary, by accepting that discipline, you become capable of listening to the intended meaning. In order to stimulate your thinking as you work from observations toward understanding the text, ask yourself some of these questions:

1. Which ideas are central to this author's vision?
2. Why are they important?
3. How do they relate to ideas taught by this author in other places?
4. What new concepts are defined by this text?
5. What am I told about God and his character?
6. What am I told about man?
7. What patterns does the author see in the relationship between God and man?

When the author wrote, he chose to include certain details and omit others in order to make a point. What is that point?

Application. The interpretative process does not end when the main point has been discovered and clarified. Paul wrote in Romans 4:23-24 that the words of the Old Testament "were written not for his [Abraham's] sake alone, but for ours also." Evangelicals confess, in imitation of Paul, that the Bible in its entirety was written for our sake. Consequently, after understanding what the text means, evangelicals go on to ask:

1. How can I apply this text to my life?
2. What attitudes of mine should change as a result of this new understanding?
3. What specific new responsibilities must I recognize?
4. What implications does this text have for my lifestyle? my career? my personal relationships?
5. What patterns should I expect to see in history or within interpersonal relationships?
6. If I am to live in obedience to God's Word, how must I grow and change?

We should ask these questions not just of ourselves, but also of the Holy Spirit who promised to use the Word to nurture our growth. He will illuminate the text for us.

It is essential to note that these three steps in interpretation cannot be reversed. How can you see what God expects of you before you have understood the meaning of the text? And how can you grasp the meaning of the text prior to seeing what it actually says? Evangelical Protestants have always confessed that the Bible is the infallible Word of God; it can be trusted to teach us the truth about God, ourselves and our relationship with God. Furthermore, evangelicals are confident that the Holy Spirit will, without fail, use the Bible to effect his own purposes in the life of the believer. One who reads carefully will come to understand and, through understanding the Word, will hear God and experience the redemptive power of the Holy Spirit.

Further Reading

Alexander, David and Pat, eds. *Eerdman's Handbook to the Bible*. Grand Rapids: Eerdmans, 1973. An illustrated guide to the Bible which includes maps, charts and background information which would be of use to the reader.

Douglas, J. D., ed. *The New Bible Dictionary*. Downers Grove, Ill.: InterVarsity Press, 1962. An excellent source for historical and cultural background, biographical information and short introductions to the books of the Bible. Contains hundreds of articles.

Grant, Robert M. *A Short History of the Interpretation of the Bible*. New York: Macmillan, 1963. The best available introduction to the subject.

Guthrie, D., and Motyer, J. A., eds. *The New Bible Commentary: Revised*. Downers Grove, Ill.: InterVarsity Press, 1970. An excellent one-volume commentary on the Bible which includes twelve general introductory articles.

Job, John B., ed. *How to Study the Bible: An Introduction to Methods of Bible Study.* Downers Grove, Ill.: InterVarsity Press, 1972. Each of the short chapters suggests a specific strategy for studying a biblical passage.

Ramm, Bernard. *Protestant Biblical Interpretation: A Textbook of Hermeneutics.* Grand Rapids: Baker Book House, 1970. An excellent introduction to and defense of the Protestant approach to interpreting the Bible. A trusted standby for many years.

Sproul, R. C. *Knowing Scripture.* Downers Grove, Ill.: InterVarsity Press, 1977. Lays the groundwork for how to study the Bible.

Stott, John R. W. *Understanding the Bible.* Glendale, Cal.: Regal, 1972. An excellent introduction written for lay people.

See also the bibliography on the Old Testament at the end of chapter four and the bibliography on the New Testament at the end of chapter five.

WHERE IT ALL BEGAN: DISCOVERING THE OLD TESTAMENT

4

"Open your booklets to page three. Ready, begin!"

The tester in charge sat down, and the scraping of pencils on paper filled the silence. A moment later a question jolted me in a way that I have never forgotten. "Place the following three kings in chronological order: Jeroboam, David, Uzziah." Place them in order? I had never even heard of two of them!

I had chosen to attend a Christian college which required all incoming freshmen to undergo a week of testing prior to registration. We were told that the results from these tests would be used to place each new student into appropriate classes. One of these tests covered the Old Testament. I went confidently to that exam for I had been brought up in a good, Bible-teaching church. I had been an officer in the youth group and had tried to study the Bible on my own. So I had assumed that I would have about as good a chance as anyone on this particular test. An hour later I left the testing room appalled at my apparent ignorance of the Old Testament.

In a few days word came back that my score had been fairly high. Due to some lucky guessing or the greater ignorance of my classmates, my score was high enough to meet the requirement in Old Testament. But when the time came to register for classes, I enrolled in the subject anyway. I needed it!

In retrospect, it is clear that my church had taught me about the Old Testament in an extremely selective way. I knew all of the stories from the book of Genesis fairly well. I could also recount the stories of Samuel's anointing of Saul, David's fight with Goliath and Joshua's battle at Jericho. But I lacked a framework. I had heard of Solomon, of course. But no one had ever told me that Solomon's empire was severely diminished by a civil war just after his death. I knew about Jonah and the whale. But I did not know that Jonah was a prophet of Israel, the larger of the two countries formed by that civil war.

This chapter is intended to give you a framework for looking at the Old Testament. Due to limitations of time and space, this will be only the roughest of outlines. But it will, I hope, enable the reader who is new to the Old Testament to venture into the book without fear of being overwhelmed.

The History of Israel
The history of Israel has as many names, dates and conflicts as any other history. But it has one characteristic which allows the beginning student to gain an overview of the subject easily. It is divided into several periods by some very obvious turning points (see the timeline on page 48). That helps a lot.

Israel's history began when Abraham, the father of the Hebrew people, heard God's command (about 2000 B.C.) to migrate from Ur of the Chaldees, a city at the tip of the Persian Gulf. God did not tell Abraham the name of his destination, but he promised to be with Abraham all the way. After God led Abraham to Palestine, he made a covenant with Abraham. He promised that Abraham would have a child in spite of his old age and that his descendants would become a mighty nation in

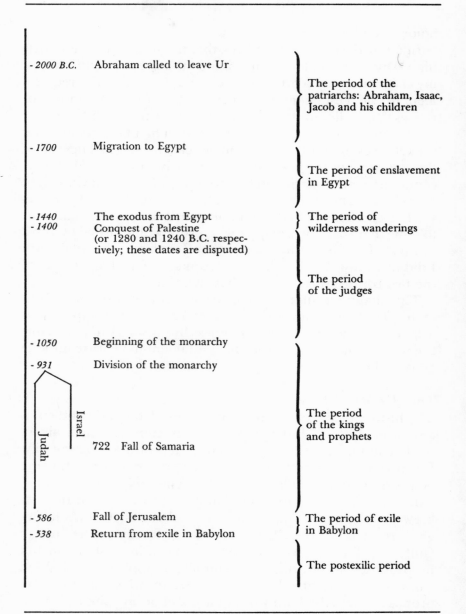

- 2000 B.C.	Abraham called to leave Ur	The period of the patriarchs: Abraham, Isaac, Jacob and his children
- 1700	Migration to Egypt	The period of enslavement in Egypt
- 1440	The exodus from Egypt	The period of wilderness wanderings
- 1400	Conquest of Palestine (or 1280 and 1240 B.C. respectively; these dates are disputed)	
		The period of the judges
- 1050	Beginning of the monarchy	
- 931	Division of the monarchy	
	Judah / Israel — 722 Fall of Samaria	The period of the kings and prophets
- 586	Fall of Jerusalem	The period of exile in Babylon
- 538	Return from exile in Babylon	
		The postexilic period

Table 1. *Timeline of the History of Israel*

the land of Palestine. Isaac, the promised child, passed the promise on to his son Jacob, whom God renamed "Israel." Israel fathered twelve sons who, according to biblical tradition, became the founders of the twelve tribal groups known as the "children of Israel."

Because of a famine in the Palestine area around 1700 B.C., Israel, his children and their families migrated to Egypt where the whole clan faded into obscurity for four hundred years. When we next catch sight of the descendants of Israel (about 1440 B.C.), they have become slaves in Egypt. At that time, God demonstrated his mighty power to them by rescuing them from bondage. To accomplish his purposes, God chose an Israelite named Moses as his servant. Under Moses' leadership, he brought the people of Israel out of Egypt and into the vicinity of Mt. Sinai. There God renewed his covenant with Israel and gave them his Law.

The Bible records that the Israelites, in spite of God's evident concern for their welfare, subsequently doubted and questioned him. Again and again, the people rebelled against both God and his Law. Consequently, God chose to allow them to wander in the desert for about forty years, until the older generation had died. Then under Joshua, Moses' successor, the Israelites crossed the Jordan river and began the conquest of Palestine, the Promised Land.

During the next two hundred years, called the "period of the judges," the Israelites lived in Palestine as an amphictyony, a loose federation of tribes gathered around a common religious shrine. In this case, the shrine was the Ark of the Covenant, an ornate chest containing the Laws given to Israel at Mt. Sinai. But in spite of the fact that they were federated around the Ark of the Covenant, they frequently ignored the stipulations of that agreement. The book of Judges states that "every man did what was right in his own eyes" (17:6). So from time to time during this period, God would raise up judges who provided political, military and (in some cases) religious leadership.

About 1050 B.C. military pressures from the Philistines, a tribal group who resided on the Mediterranean Sea, forced the people of Israel to establish a monarchy. The first three kings—Saul (1050-1010), David (1010-970) and Solomon (970-931)—are among the most famous personages of the Old Testament. Saul and David dealt with the military threat. Early in his reign, David conquered Jerusalem and then centralized both the government and the religious life of the people there. Because of the stability of David's reign, his son Solomon reigned in an era of unequaled prosperity.

Following the death of Solomon in 931 B.C., civil war divided the people of Israel into two countries. Judah, which occupied the southern part of the original territory, continued to accept Davidic rule. But a majority of the tribes separated from Judah to form a larger kingdom, called Israel, in the north. The histories of Judah and Israel for the next three hundred fifty years read much like any other history from the ancient period. There are petty rivalries, border wars and alliances. Yet out of these two countries during this period came the prophetic literature of the Old Testament. This is what gives distinction to these two tiny countries which otherwise would have slipped into obscurity.

This period of history ends with political disaster. After a long religious decline and a corresponding political decline, Israel was destroyed by the Assyrians in 722 B.C. After the fall of Samaria, the capital city of Israel, the aristocracy was taken into exile. Israel faded from history as the conquered intermingled with the conquerors. Judah managed to last somewhat longer (until 586 B.C.), but it too fell when the Babylonians destroyed Jerusalem. In imitation of the Assyrians, the Babylonians took the aristocracy of Judah into exile. But in this case the exile was not the beginning of the end.

The destruction of Jerusalem caused a national trauma, which was what God intended it to do. By this crisis he forced the Jewish people to re-examine their understanding of the covenants which God had made with them. If the destruction of Jerusalem accomplished nothing more, it convinced the Jewish people that God valued neither the temple and its worship nor their political independence as much as they did.

About fifty years later (539 B.C.), Babylon itself was conquered by the Persians, a more tolerant people. The following year the Jews were allowed to return to Palestine. This small exodus began the postexilic period. Judah was re-established, but only as a province within the Persian empire. In time the temple was even rebuilt in Jerusalem, but it stood as a bitter-sweet and permanent reminder of the greater glories of the one built by Solomon and destroyed by the Babylonians. The exile experience was not without significance. Through it the Jews learned the importance of keeping the Law.

The Books of the Old Testament

What has been said so far by way of an overview of Israel's history differs little in form from an overview of the history of any minor nation. It would be impossible to understand the Old Testament without some sense for such details. But for the Christian student of the Old Testament, the history of Israel remains a secondary interest. The literature of the Old Testament, the Word itself and the theology which is taught in that literature occupy the center of attention.

My purpose here is to introduce the books of the Old Testament. But beyond that, I hope that you will become intrigued enough with the Old Testament to read it. One hears occasionally of a new Christian who began to read through the Old Testament only to get bogged down in some long, dry-as-dust section. If you understand how the Old Testament is put together, you are not so likely to have that experience.

The books of the Old Testament are not arranged chronologically. Rather they are grouped by their literary form, as Table 2 shows. Within each group—except poetry—the books are arranged in a very rough chronological sequence. And the prophets and poetry overlap the historical books.

The five books of Moses. The first section of the Old Testament is called the *Law*. The Hebrew word, *torah*, which is usually translated as "law," really means "instruction." The idea is a good deal broader than just "legal ordinances." When the ancient Hebrews spoke of the Law, they made no clear distinction, as we would, between the moral law, the legal code for governing society, and the ritual law for the regulation of the rather complex Hebrew worship. Since the Hebrews did not, quite literally, perceive the distinctions, they mixed all of these laws together into a composite description of how the people of God were to live as a covenant people. In its primary sense then, the Law is the sum of all the laws which define our responsibility to God and our neighbors. In a derived sense, it refers to the five books which contain the Law. But of course these books contain much more than just laws. They include history, biography, poetry and some genealogies.

The Bible begins with these five books of the Law. The first quarter of the book of Genesis contains some of the most famous stories of the Bible such as the creation, the Fall, the flood and the tower of Babel. The rest of the book recounts the stories of the Patriarchs: Abraham, Isaac, Jacob and Jacob's sons, espe-

Law	History	Poetry	Minor Prophets
Genesis	Joshua	Job	Hosea
Exodus	Judges	Psalms	Joel
Leviticus	Ruth	Proverbs	Amos
Numbers	1 Samuel	Ecclesiastes	Obadiah
Deuteronomy	2 Samuel	Song of Solomon	Jonah
	1 Kings		Micah
	2 Kings	**Major Prophets**	Nahum
	1 Chronicles	Isaiah	Habakkuk
	2 Chronicles	Jeremiah	Zephaniah
	Ezra	Lamentations	Haggai
	Nehemiah	Ezekiel	Zechariah
	Esther	Daniel	Malachi

Table 2. *The Books of the Old Testament*

cially Joseph. There are no legal sections as such in Genesis, although there is much instruction for the attentive reader. The book of Exodus picks up the story about four hundred years later, at the time of Moses. It tells how God liberated his people from bondage in Egypt, how he made the covenant with them at Sinai, and how the tabernacle was to be constructed. (The tabernacle was Israel's portable house of worship during their wilderness wanderings.)

These two books, Genesis and Exodus, contain some of the most theologically significant passages in the whole Old Testament. They are clear enough for even the beginning student. But the third book of the Law, Leviticus, is likely to discourage all but the most dedicated students of the Bible. It provides detailed instructions regarding the forms of worship which God prescribed. It delineates what sacrifices were to be offered, how the tabernacle was to be operated, and how the priesthood was supposed to function. People who try to read the Bible "from cover to cover" have an unfortunate tendency to abandon the project in Leviticus. It is advisable to master some of the more central books first.

The book of Numbers records additional laws and recounts the history of the Hebrew people from Sinai to the outskirts of the Promised Land. Deuteronomy (the word means "second law") records the farewell addresses of Moses in which he reviewed the history of God's relationship with the people of Israel up to that point and the nature of their covenant relationship.

The historical books. The second section of the Old Testament contains two distinct accounts of the history of Israel. The first of these accounts is contained in Joshua, Judges, 1 and 2 Samuel, and 1 and 2 Kings. In the Hebrew Bible these books are known as the "former prophets," a designation which recognizes that they are not merely a record of Israel's history. They are, rather, an interpretation of that history from the perspective of Israel's prophets.

Most people think of history as a presentation of the facts. But those who write history know better. There are always too many facts to record, so historians must omit some and include others. These decisions place the writer's own personal stamp on the document. His or her subjective assessment of which facts are important determines what is written. When historians decide how to arrange the selected facts, subjectivity again enters the picture. No historian presents, nor can present, a truly objective report of events. The biblical historians were no exception. As *prophetic* historians, they knew that God was very much involved in the history of Israel and that Israel's response to the covenant affected the political stability of the nation (for example, read the book of Judges). Their histories reflect this prophetic interpretation of Israel's destiny. Thus, they are indeed the former *prophets*.

The second account of the history of Israel, which includes 1 and 2 Chronicles, Ezra and Nehemiah, was written much later. While the first account, the "former prophets," takes the story of Israel from the death of Moses to the Babylonian exile, this second account takes the reader from David (after a very condensed review of all of Israel's previous history) into the postexilic period. (You may wish to refer again to Tables 1 and 2.)

The poetic books. Although the third section of the Old Testament is normally called "poetry," "literature" might be closer to the mark. The book of Psalms, a collection of Hebrew poetry, has always been one of the best-loved sections of the Bible. Most of the individual poems it contains are hymns which were sung by the people of Israel at the temple in Jerusalem.

The Hebrew poetry contained in the Psalms does not rhyme, as English poetry frequently does. The Hebrews often used instead a poetic device known as parallelism. Two consecutive lines of Hebrew poetry will frequently repeat an idea in almost identical words. For example Psalm 19:1 begins, "The heavens are telling the glory of God; and the firmament proclaims his handiwork." Hebrew parallelism was not written to communicate subtle shades of meaning. It was utilized in order to express a particular idea beautifully. So the reader should look for the central idea of a couplet and enjoy the rhythm of its parallel expression.

Song of Solomon, a second and *much* shorter collection of poetry, extols the love of a man and a woman for each other. Jewish interpreters take it to be a picture of the love of Yahweh for Israel. The church has usually seen the love of Christ for his church portrayed in the book.

Three other books in the poetic section—Job, Proverbs, and Ecclesiastes—should be classed as wisdom literature, a literary genre which was typical of the ancient Near East. In the ancient world, kings frequently had literary men within their courts who collected and wrote so-called wise sayings. These sayings were used to instruct the young in reading and writing while at the same time imparting wisdom on how to live successfully. Similar reading texts have been used through the years in the United States to teach morals as well as English.

In the Old Testament there are three distinct varieties of this wisdom literature. Proverbs contains hundreds of short, pithy sayings on how to live wisely. The book of Job is a dialog between Job and three friends on the question, Why do people suffer? Ecclesiastes is a monolog on the nature of the good life. The fact that the Jews of the Old Testament wrote wisdom literature, just as did other peoples in the ancient Near East, illustrates again how God used human structures when he revealed his Word to us. The Hebrew poets, however, made one distinct contribution to the concept of wisdom. They wrote, "The fear of the LORD is the beginning of wisdom" (Prov. 9:10).

The Prophets. The section called the "Prophets" includes seventeen books in all which are usually divided into the major prophets and the minor prophets. This distinction is frequently taken to mean "important" and "unimportant," a most unfortunate designation. Originally this distinction was based solely on the length of the books. All twelve of the minor prophets fit nicely onto one scroll, so they were kept together strictly as a convenience. These so-called minor prophets are most certainly not minor in importance. In fact, the book written by the minor prophet Amos is an excellent place to begin reading the prophets. This book is short and relatively easy to comprehend. And the message is definitely relevant to the contemporary American scene.

The English word *prophecy* most frequently means "foretelling the future." There is certainly an element of that in the prophets, but biblical prophecy is not solely *fore*telling. In most of the prophetic literature we see the prophets *forth*telling the Word of God. This means that the prophets used the revelation that God had given to them and their knowledge of how he acts within history to interpret the flow of history to people who had forgotten the covenant. They frequently spoke of the need for justice and mercy within society (forthtelling) and predicted doom on Israel for ignoring such needs (foretelling). For the prophets, forthtelling and foretelling were related in that both stemmed from their vision of God and from the Word of God which had been given to them. If God is the same today as he was then—and evangelicals are convinced that he is—then the way God acted in their history can speak with power to us now.

Basic Old Testament Doctrines

The Old Testament is a very concrete, down-to-earth sort of book. In it you will find stories of all kinds of interesting people, descriptions of the laws which governed Israel during their desert wanderings, and examples of prophetic preaching originally directed to some very specific situation. You will not find a passage which neatly sums up the theology of the Old Testament. The book does not even spell out the doctrine of God or the doctrine of salvation in any detail. So when we turn to this book, we must look for theological ideas woven in and through the very texture of the Old Testament account. A few concepts, however, crop up continually in the Old Testament, and a knowledge of these will aid readers on their journeys into the Old Testament world.

God. The Hebrew religion began with the assumption that a God who utterly transcends this world does, in actual fact, exist.

The people knew this God as "Yahweh" ("Jehovah"). The word comes from the Hebrew verb meaning "to be." Yahweh is, then, "the one who is" or perhaps "the one who causes to be." It was Yahweh who created the world. While that may seem like a simple idea, it would be hard to find one more pregnant with implications.

There is a good deal of disagreement within the evangelical community on how to interpret the creation stories, but on one point there is absolute agreement. Whenever and however the world came into being, it was not a cosmic accident. There can be no compromise with naturalism on this point. God was the active agent in creation. And when we shift our focus to the relation between Christianity and other world religions, this doctrine remains central in the discussion. More than anything else, it is this absolute distinction between the creator and the created which sets the religion of the Old Testament apart from all of the Eastern traditions.

God, the eternally creative One, chose not to remain alone. He chose to make man in his own image and to enter into relationship with him. Subsequently, man and woman rebelled against God and so fell into sin. But, according to the Genesis story, even while they were hiding from God, God was seeking them in an effort to mend the broken relationship. The almighty God of the Old Testament led the way in re-establishing the relationship. And even more important, he continues to take the initiative in rebuilding communication with each person.

This same pattern is visible in the relationship between God and the people of Israel. God chose Israel to be his people, called her out of Egypt, made a covenant with her and brought her into the Promised Land. But Israel did not remain faithful to the covenant. The prophet Hosea expresses God's grief over Israel, picturing her as a wayward son. "When Israel was a child, I loved him, and out of Egypt I called my son. The more I called them, the more they went from me; . . . It was I who taught Ephraim to walk, I took them up in my arms; . . . They shall return to the land of Egypt, and Assyria shall be their king, because they have refused to return to me" (Hos. 11:1-3, 5). Precisely because God loved Israel he was willing to send her into exile for being unfaithful to the covenant. Only through such discipline could Israel be purified for a renewed relationship. Yahweh is a God of love, and his love is holy and jealous.

People commonly say that the God of the New Testament is a loving father, but the God of the Old Testament is a God of vengeance. Nothing could be further from the truth. The Old Testament frequently portrays God as stern or wrathful, but these are not the only aspects of his character. They are not even the dominant ones. How could God show love to a disobedient Israel if not by being stern? On the contrary, the Old Testament shows quite clearly that one of the basic elements in God's character is his openness to and desire for a relationship with man.

Humanity. The human race, from one perspective, is a part of creation. People are joined with the animals, plants and all the other elements of earth. But from another perspective, human beings are infinitely removed from the rest of creation. When God made the first human beings, he created them in his own image. Like God, they were capable of creative acts and personal relationships. When the man and woman chose to sin, they alienated themselves from God. But in spite of this, they and their descendants retained their value to God; humanity continues to bear his image.

Sin. The Old Testament speaks much of sin, yet this concept is frequently misunderstood. In the Old Testament, God forbade certain actions such as theft, murder and covetousness. But these prohibitions are not the arbitrary rules of a hostile God. They are, on the contrary, expressions of God's very character. To murder is destructive. It destroys life rather than creates it. Furthermore, the act permanently alienates the murderer from the person who is killed. There is no longer the possibility of reconciliation. As a destructive, alienating action, it is a repudiation of God's character. This is why murder is wrong.

The same analysis explains the commandment against adultery. Marriages have value. So God was saying, in effect, "Do not destroy someone's marriage. Do not be the one who causes alienation between a husband and a wife." When people sin, they are changed. They become destructive, and their destructive conduct alienates them from themselves, from other people and from God. All of the relationships which God intended people to have are twisted by sin. In the act of sin, people side with destruction and alienation. At its most basic level, sin is a rejection of God.

Salvation. If in the Old Testament sin was not merely "breaking the rules," so also salvation was not gained by merely "keeping the rules." God never demanded obedience to his commandments as a precondition for the covenant relationship. The commandments were given to Israel *after* the covenant was established. Evangelicals see this pattern as the key to a proper relationship with God. Salvation is life within a covenant relationship. The commandments were given as a guide to the proper response to that relationship. This concept unlocks the prophetic message. The prophets insisted that disobedience to the commandments of the covenant constituted a repudiation of the covenant relationship. One could not then—any more than now—live in a relationship with God while being disobedient to the commandments. But the call was not merely to a renewed obedience to the stipulations of the covenant. It was also primarily a call to renew the covenant relationship itself.

Getting Started
You may be familiar with the doctrine which asserts that the Old Testament is fulfilled in the New Testament. This means that the problems and expectations which were raised by the events recounted in the Old Testament have been solved and realized in the New. This idea might lead you to ask, "If the Old Testament is fulfilled in the New, then why not just ignore the Old?" The question is a good one, but the answer is quite simple. While it is true that there was an *old* covenant, and that there is now a *new* covenant, the God who offers to live with man-

kind in a covenant relationship is still the same. God's effort to bring salvation to all people, which culminated in Jesus Christ, began in the Old Testament. To understand Jesus fully one must know the Old Testament well enough to be able to see him as the fulfillment. In short, the study of the Old Testament will deepen your understanding of God and the salvation he offers to us through Jesus Christ.

Where in the Old Testament should you begin reading? Let me suggest five books to start: Genesis, Exodus, Judges, Psalms and Amos. These books span almost the entire history of Israel and include all of the major literary forms found in the Old Testament. In each book you will see a particular facet of God's nature and of his efforts to recreate his relationship with all people to bring salvation to them. This makes each of the books worth reading.

Further Reading

Bright, John. *A History of Israel.* Philadelphia: Westminster Press, 1972. A standard history of Israel from Abraham to the intertestamental period.

Douglas, J. D., ed. *The New Bible Dictionary.* Downers Grove, Ill.: InterVarsity Press, 1962. A good source for information on specific topics.

Ellison, Henry L. *The Message of the Old Testament.* Grand Rapids: Eerdmans, 1969. A brief, lucid exposition on the theology of the Old Testament.

Schultz, Samuel. *The Old Testament Speaks: Old Testament History and Literature.* New York: Harper & Row, 1970. A widely used evangelical textbook.

WHERE IT ALL LEADS: UNDERSTANDING THE NEW TESTAMENT

5

In the Old Testament we have a record of the beginnings of our Christian family. True, the word *Christian* does not even appear in the Old Testament, to say nothing of the word *evangelical*. Nonetheless that is where the roots of our faith began. When we reach the New Testament, we are much closer to home, for the terms *church* and *Christian* first appear there. The New Testament records the life and work of Jesus, the Christ, as well as the birth and early development of the Christian church. Here we read of how God reconciled the human race with himself.

New Testament Times
Between the Testaments. After their return from exile in Babylon in 538 B.C., the Jews lived in Palestine under the control of the Persian empire for about the next two hundred years. In 331 Alexander the Great destroyed Persian power and brought Palestine under Greek influence. After Alexander died, Palestine existed under the domination of the Ptolomies of Egypt for

another hundred years (until 198 B.C.) and after that under Syrian control for a generation. Then in 167 B.C., the Jews, under the leadership of the Maccabean family, revolted against the Seleucids, the ruling family of Syria. The events of the following hundred years are so tangled that only a historian of the period would have the devotion to unravel them. Palestine was torn by guerrilla warfare. Plots and counterplots, rulers and pretenders to the throne crowd the scene. But the chaos ended in 63 B.C. when Pompey established Roman rule in Palestine (or "Judea" as the country came to be called under the Romans). For our purposes, the story really gets interesting when Herod was appointed King of Judea in 37 B.C.

Judea at the time of Christ. Herod the Great was the king that the wise men visited in the biblical accounts of the birth of Jesus (Mt. 1:18—2:23; Lk. 1:26—2:20). As you can see from the text of Matthew, Herod was a cruel ruler. After his death in 4 B.C., Herod's kingdom was split up among his sons. The area of "Judea proper" (the land directly west of the Dead Sea) was given to his eldest son, Archelaus. The Romans removed Archelaus in A.D. 6 because of his gross mismanagement and replaced him with a provincial governor ("procurator"). Pontius Pilate held that position from A.D. 26-36. As procurator he became involved in the trial of Jesus.

Another of Herod's sons, Herod Antipas, was given control over Galilee (a part of the country of Judea which lies north of Judea proper, between the Sea of Galilee and the Mediterranean Sea). Herod Antipas ruled until A.D. 39. The Bible refers to both Herod Antipas and his father, Herod the Great, as "Herod." Whenever Herod is mentioned in conjunction with Jesus' ministry, the reference is (with but one unimportant exception) to the *son* of Herod the Great.

During the time of Jesus' ministry, around A.D. 30, the Romans ruled over all of Judea. Herod Antipas ruled Galilee and Pontius Pilate governed Judea proper. Both ruled at the pleasure of the Roman Senate. A knowledge of the internal political and religious situation in Judea at this time will clarify the subtle conflicts recorded in the Gospels.

As procurator, Pilate had two major areas of responsibility—civil order and taxation. Civil order was maintained in two ways. First of all, Pilate had a body of Roman soldiers at his disposal for any necessary police action and for administering the death penalty for serious crimes. Second, the Jews governed themselves for the most part through their "Great Council" or "Sanhedrin." The Sanhedrin consisted of seventy Jewish men who acted as a kind of Supreme Court and Congress rolled into one. Because of their important legal responsibilities, many of the men who sat on the Sanhedrin would have been scribes (lawyers).

Tax collection, the other half of Pilate's responsibility, was carried out by a kind of franchise operation. Appointed individuals were allowed to collect taxes in specified areas. They were required to pay a certain amount to the Roman government for that privilege, but anything over and above the agreed-upon amount was theirs to keep. In addition, these tax collectors were allowed to created subfranchise areas within their jurisdiction. The whole operation was very lucrative for those who cooperated. Not too surprisingly, however, Jews who accepted such a position were considered traitors to their people. As such, they were at the bottom of the social heap. In fact, the Gospels sometimes speak of "sinners and tax collectors."

There were among the Jews at this time two major political parties, the Herodians and the Zealots. These parties were not official in any way; that is, they were not formally recognized the way political parties are in the United States. The Herodians believed that the status quo was the best that could be hoped for. The Herods, they pointed out, were at least partially Jewish, and the Jews had religious freedom and some degree of home rule under the Romans. From their point of view, things could have been a lot worse. The Zealots disagreed. They argued that religious freedom is never enough. The Romans could revoke that just as the Seleucids had done earlier. To be truly free, people must have political freedom as well. The tension between these two points of view was still mild at the time of Jesus' ministry, but occasionally the political perspective of Jesus' listeners colored their reactions to him. The Herodians feared that Jesus' talk about the kingdom would stir up trouble. The Zealots hoped it would. Both groups agreed, however, that religious values held precedence over political ones.

In the Gospel accounts two religious groups, the Sadducees and the Pharisees, are in constant conflict with each other and with Jesus. The Sadducees took a strict approach to the Law. They emphasized the liturgy and the ritual of Temple worship precisely because it was explicitly taught in the Old Testament. Because the Old Testament did not seem to teach the possibility of a future life, for example, they denied the doctrine of the resurrection of the dead. They were, therefore, the conservatives or literalists of the period. The Pharisees, on the other hand, were willing to accept some of these newer interpretations and doctrines, but they were most distinctive in their emphasis on personal piety. They believed that God had sent Israel into exile in Babylon for her disobedience to the Law. Hence they insisted that all of Israel, both as individuals and as a corporate body, needed to be extremely scrupulous in keeping the details of the Law. Many of them believed that if all of Israel were to keep the Sabbath for two consecutive weeks, then the Messiah would come.

The typical Jew would have belonged to neither party although he or she would have been careful to fulfill religious obligations. On the important festivals, such as Passover, he might attend the temple in Jerusalem where the ritual delineated in the Old Testament Law was scrupulously carried out. Most of the time, however, he would have worshiped near his home, in a building called a synagogue. These buildings were set aside for Sabbath worship, study of the Scriptures and prayer. Synagogues were a necessity in outlying areas, but were common even in Jerusalem.

Around A.D. 40, after Jesus' death and resurrection, the whole of Judea was reunited under a third Herod, Herod

Agrippa I. His reign was brief, lasting only until A.D. 44. There-after the country of Judea was again placed under a Roman procurator. After about A.D. 50, Zealot activity intensified and Judea gradually slid into revolt. In A.D. 66, the Romans were forced to move in troops to suppress an open rebellion in the Jewish state. The reconquest took much longer than expected. The Jews were stubborn fighters. But eventually, in A.D. 70, Jerusalem fell to the Romans and the temple was destroyed (as Jesus had warned it would be).

The beginnings of the Christian church. Christianity is considered to have separated itself from Judaism on the day of the Feast of Pentecost in the year that Jesus was crucified (about A.D. 30). Throughout the Old Testament God had taken the initiative toward mankind. That pattern of divine initiative had climaxed in Jesus Christ. God himself entered history and became a man. But the Jewish people had not understood, and Jesus was exe-cuted. He rose from the dead and ascended into heaven. Ten days after the ascension, the disciples were in Jerusalem as Jesus had commanded, but they were disorganized and confused about what he expected of them. Then a totally unexpected event occurred. The Holy Spirit descended upon them and bestowed on them the power that Christ himself had promised. The day of Pentecost became the beginning of a new phase in God's plan of redemption.

In the days and months which followed this tremendous event, the Christian movement experienced a remarkable burst of growth. Because of this, it became the object of Jewish per-secution. Christians were forced to leave Judea, but as they did they formed new churches in nearby Roman population centers. This proximity to Gentiles, however, immediately raised a ques-tion for the young church. Was the gospel, the good news about Jesus, intended for the Jews alone or was it also for Gentiles? The book of Acts records the story of how Peter was led by God to preach to a Roman centurion named Cornelius (Acts 10). This event set a precedent, and soon the gospel was spreading rapidly throughout the gentile world.

The ministry of Paul. Much of the early growth of the church was directed and encouraged by disciples commissioned at Pentecost. But probably the single strongest impetus for the gospel came from a man who never met Jesus during his public ministry. Sometime about A.D. 32 Saul of Tarsus, a leader of the Pharisees, was traveling to Damascus to direct the persecution of the Christians there. On that trip he had a vision of the Lord Jesus who confronted him with his own guilt as the persecutor of the young Christian movement (see Acts 9:1-19). The vision turned him from his plans. He converted to the Christian faith and accepted his call from the Lord to be the apostle to the Gentiles. Later, around A.D. 45, Saul (now called Paul) helped with the ministry in Antioch. Later still, the church was guided by the Holy Spirit to commission him to lead the first company of missionaries.

With the conversion of more and more Gentiles the issue of their place in the church threatened to split the Christians. Some of the Jewish Christians felt that all converts should be required to keep the full Old Testament Law (including circumcision and the dietary laws). Others, particularly Paul, disagreed. They asserted that the Law was given by God to the Jews alone. When the problem came to a head in Antioch, it was referred to the apostles in Jerusalem. After much debate they decreed that the Gentiles were under no obligation to keep the Law. In so doing they vindicated Paul's preaching.

Their decision effectively opened the way for the rapid spread of the gospel. During the next twenty years, Paul traveled widely throughout the eastern Mediterranean area, spreading the good news about the resurrection of Jesus and writing to the churches he founded. According to tradition, he died during the Neronian persecutions in A.D. 64 after several years of imprisonment.

During the last third of the century, the church solidified her position in spite of occasional periods of persecution by the Roman government. The Gospels which would eventually become part of the New Testament began to appear and circulate along with Paul's letters. The church took on a more fixed form for its worship and ministry. Several incipient heresies began to make inroads into the church, and the church took the first steps to clarify her teaching in response to them.

The Books of the New Testament
The books of the New Testament, like the Old, are not organized by chronology but grouped by literary form into history, letters by Paul, general letters and the like. We also meet a completely unique genre of literature called "gospel." The word means "good news" and that is terribly important. The gospel is not a philosophy nor merely a set of moral values. Fundamentally, it is news and in particular *good* news. The gospel is the proclamation that God became a man in the person of Jesus of Nazareth in order to free us from the power of sin. It includes the story of his death for us and his victory over death.

The Gospels. The Gospels (Matthew, Mark, Luke and John—traditionally named for their authors) recount that story. These particular books are certainly not biographies, for they deal with only a fraction of Jesus' life. Two of the Gospels, in fact, are completely silent about the first thirty years of his life. No book which omits that much of a person's life can possibly be construed as biography. They do, however, provide a historical record of the central events of the life and ministry of Jesus. They recount his teachings and his miracles. They tell us about his attitudes toward himself, his Father and those around him. The Gospels focus their attention on Jesus' death and resurrection. Therefore they might best be called "theological interpretations of the life, death and resurrection of Jesus."

The first three Gospels are frequently called the "synoptic Gospels" because they have a marked similarity in content and approach to the life of Jesus. Most evangelical scholars today believe that Matthew and Luke made some use of Mark's Gospel, which accounts for some of the overlap. In their record of Jesus' ministry in Galilee, the synoptics emphasize the miracles of Jesus, his frequent clashes with demonic powers and his parables.

The Gospels	The Letters of Paul	The General Letters
Matthew	Romans	Hebrews
Mark	1 Corinthians	James
Luke	2 Corinthians	1 Peter
John	Galatians	2 Peter
	Ephesians	1 John
History	Philippians	2 John
Acts	Colossians	3 John
	1 Thessalonians	Jude
	2 Thessalonians	
	1 Timothy	The Revelation of John
	2 Timothy	
	Titus	
	Philemon	

Table 3. *The Books of the New Testament*

Since Matthew quotes extensively from the Old Testament and shows Jesus as the fulfillment of prophecy, it was probably written as an explanation of the gospel for the Jews. Mark shows Jesus as an active, vigorous and decisive leader. According to tradition, this book was written in Rome and represents Mark's summary of the teaching and preaching of the apostle Peter. Luke was written by a gentile doctor who accompanied Paul on some of his missionary journeys. His Gospel emphasizes the importance of prayer and the work of the Holy Spirit, and Jesus' concern for women and Gentiles.

John, the fourth Gospel, ushers the reader into a totally new kind of literary environment. Where the synoptics emphasize Jesus' ministry in Galilee, John emphasizes Jesus' visits to Jerusalem for the feast days. While the teachings of Jesus in the synoptics are normally contained in short, pithy statements, Jesus' discourses as recorded by John are considerably longer and much more philosophical in tone. In the synoptics, Jesus speaks of himself as the Son of man and teaches about the kingdom of God. John sees Jesus as the Christ, the Son of God, and writes about faith and receiving eternal life.

The four interpretations of the life of Jesus contained in the

Gospels represent the various ways in which the four authors understood him. Through the inspiration of the Holy Spirit, we have four distinct portraits of Jesus. The contrasts between the various perspectives can create difficulties for the interpreter. Yet, when each of the four Gospels is allowed to speak its message, when the integrity of each Gospel is respected, the differing perspectives can add depth to our understanding of our Savior.

History. The Acts of the Apostles begins with the ascension of Jesus and tells the story of the growth and development of the early church. It is, therefore, placed just after the four Gospels in the New Testament. Luke, the Gospel writer, probably wrote Acts as the second volume of his account of the origins of the Christian faith. It ends abruptly with Paul in prison in Rome and the outcome of his case in doubt. The text offers no explanation for its abrupt end, but some have conjectured that Luke planned to continue Acts at a later date and was prevented from doing so. Others have surmised that he hoped to add a third volume. In any case, Acts should be read as a continuation of Luke even though the two books do not stand together in the New Testament.

In Acts Luke's concern for the Gentiles becomes a dominant theme. Before his ascension Jesus promised to send his Holy Spirit to direct Jesus' followers to proclaim the gospel in Jerusalem, Judea, Samaria and to all parts of the world. That sequence summarizes the chronology of Acts fairly well. The book first recounts the history of the church during the first ten years or so. At this time many Christians were still living in Jerusalem, and Peter was still playing a prominent role there. Acts records the first persecutions and the spread of Christianity into the surrounding area. We see how the gospel message first reached Samaria, and we meet Cornelius, the first gentile convert to the Christian faith. Next we read of the conversion of Paul. The remainder of the book records the gentile mission; that is, Paul's four missionary journeys throughout the Mediterranean and southeastern Europe. Acts is the only book in the New Testament which chronicles the birth and early years of the church.

The letters of Paul. The rest of the New Testament contains a collection of letters ("epistles"), many of which were written by the apostle Paul. Paul's letters are arranged in order of their length, from Romans (the longest) to Philemon (the shortest). They are named after the recipient church or individual. Paul, for example, wrote a letter to the church in Corinth on at least two occasions. Hence the New Testament contains both a 1 Corinthians and a 2 Corinthians.

In his writings Paul used the accepted form for a letter in the Greek world. He introduced himself and then named his recipients and offered a prayer on their behalf. He closed with personal greetings and a brief doxology (statement of praise to God). The body of Paul's letters almost always begins with a doctrinal statement and then moves on to practical, ethical guidance about how to apply the doctrine. Most of the letters were prompted by a particular need on a particular occasion. This means that knowledge of both the general historical background and the particular situation of the recipient will usually enhance the reader's understanding of Paul's line of thought. This information can be obtained from a Bible commentary or a New Testament survey (see pp. 44 and 77).

Paul's letter to the Romans is the nearest thing in the Bible to a systematic essay on theology. In the Bible, theology is normally implicit. The theology comes through the way the writers interpret the events they narrate. While all of Paul's letters are theological in orientation, most of what he wrote was directed to a particular church with a particular question or problem. His letters represented a deeply felt response to some particular historical situation. Romans is the exception. Paul makes no special reference to the state of affairs in the Roman church because he had never visited that church before he wrote. In this book his theology is explicit. Because of this, Romans has always been foundational for understanding the rest of Paul's work. It elucidates ideas that come up elsewhere with less clarity.

In 1 Corinthians Paul responds to a series of questions sent to him by someone in the Corinthian church. His replies embody and illustrate principles which, if applied, will enable any church to grow into good health.

The third of Paul's letters that I would especially recommend is Galatians. This brief, but fiery tract attacks the teachings of the Judaizers—a group of Christian Pharisees from Jerusalem who wished to impose Hebrew Law on gentile converts. Since legalism (the effort to define Christian behavior by a set of rules) is a recurring problem in the church, Paul's rebuttal and his theology of freedom provide a core of values to help new Christians. Of the thirteen letters traditionally attributed to Paul, these three are in my opinion the "best of Paul" and provide a good introduction to his writings.

The non-Pauline letters. The letters in the New Testament canon not written by Paul are called the general letters. Like the Pauline letters, they are arranged in the New Testament according to their length, beginning with the longest. Except for Hebrews, an anonymous book written to Jewish Christians, each of these letters is named after its respective author, rather than after the recipient. The typological approach to the Old Testament used in Hebrews and its concern to show the superiority of the gospel over the Old Covenant suggest that it was written to a group of Jewish Christians who were having second thoughts about their conversion.

The letter of James discusses the importance of having a faith which works itself out in an ethical life. On the surface it might appear to belittle Paul's doctrine of salvation by faith alone. But the contradiction is only apparent. The letter by James plays an important role in the New Testament. It forces the reader to come to a balanced understanding of Paul's theology.

The first letter of John, the Gospel writer, though only a few pages in length, is one of the most winsome and beloved writings in the Bible. In it he speaks about the importance of love and obedience to Christ.

The final book of the New Testament is called by two names: The Revelation of John and The Apocalypse. (The Greek word for *revelation* is *apocalypsis.*) The title in either language is appropriate because revelation is an excellent example of the apocalyptic literary form. The book portrays God as breaking directly into history in order to bring about the final consummation of the ages. It is by far the most symbolic book in the Bible, which makes it rather typical of its genre. For that very reason it is one of the hardest books in the whole Bible to interpret. Many New Testament commentators hold that the significance of much of its symbolism has been lost. Nonetheless, the main point of the book is absolutely clear. Revelation teaches that God will triumph over the forces of evil. The outcome of history is not now and never has been in doubt. We can assert that with absolute assurance even though problems in interpreting the symbols used in the book limit our understanding of the details. Perhaps the best way to read the book for the first time is to look for glimpses of our Lord in glory and to sense the awe that bathes the book. The interpretation of details should be left until the more basic books of the New Testament have been studied thoroughly.

Basic New Testament Doctrines

In one sense there are as many theologies in the New Testament as there are writers; that is, each author has a unique perspective on Jesus and what he accomplished. The portraits are, nonetheless, compatible. We could discuss the elements which are common to all of the writers. But investigating the divergent emphases of the various writers may bring out more of the richness of thought which is expressed in the New Testament. Therefore, we will look at the synoptic Gospels as a unit and then turn to the theologies of John and Paul.

In the synoptic Gospels. Two phrases from the synoptic Gospels, "the kingdom of God" (or "kingdom of heaven") and "the Son of man," occur so frequently and carry so much theological meaning that they provide a convenient entry into these books. The former phrases are used by all three of the Gospel writers as an introduction to Jesus' ministry. "The kingdom of God is at hand; repent, and believe in the gospel" (Mk. 1:15).

The Jewish rabbis of the period taught that history could be divided into two ages, "this age" and "the age to come." Since they thought that God would actually be present in history during the "age to come," Jesus' proclamation of the kingdom aroused some wild expectations. At one point, in fact, the people tried to make him King. But Jesus taught that the kingdom had arrived with the beginning of his public ministry. Ever since, it has existed wherever men and women give their allegiance to God, wherever they proclaim Christ as King. Still, Jesus' teaching regarding the kingdom did not exclude a future, more public manifestation of it. Jesus clearly asserted that God would indeed break into history visibly at some future point. Both teachings are true. New Testament scholars frequently explain these two understandings of the kingdom by speaking of an "overlapping of the ages." Jesus initiated the kingdom of God in his public ministry, but he will assert his kingly authority more completely at some point in the future.

The crowds around Jesus often did not understand the meaning of the kingdom. In fact, it is still hard to understand. But Jesus' teaching makes it clear that entering the kingdom is not a physical act, at least not for now. A person becomes a member of the kingdom only by responding to the message, turning from sin and choosing, in a decisive way, to give allegiance to the King. For one listener mentioned in the synoptics, that meant giving up wealth; for others, it meant something entirely different. For all people it means turning aside from whatever has been valued too highly and choosing without reservation to honor Christ, the King.

Jesus usually referred to himself as the "Son of man." Most people are aware that according to Christian doctrine, Jesus is supposed to be both God and man. So the titles "Son of God" and "Son of man" are frequently taken to reflect that idea. This is an unfortunate mistake. Jesus apparently chose the title "Son of man" in order to avoid creating confusion among his followers. The people expected the Messiah, but they pictured the

Messiah as a political leader who would free them from Roman domination. Jesus was that expected Messiah. But he was in a double bind because he refused to live up to false expectations. If he acknowledged being the Messiah, the people would expect him to lead a revolution. On the other hand, he could not deny being the Messiah without misleading them. They would want to know when the real Messiah was coming.

Jesus solved the problem by choosing a less familiar phrase, the "Son of man." A few writers just prior to the time of Jesus used that phrase to refer to a divine figure who would break into time and space from the heavens in order to initiate the kingdom. Those particular writers would not have been widely known. So Jesus was able to utilize the phrase and shape its meaning through his own usage. Jesus used the title to point to his divine status and his right to speak for God. He did not use it, as some assume, to refer to his humanity. In the account of Mark, for example, the Son of man is shown to be able to forgive sin. Jesus also taught that the Son of man must suffer, an idea which would not have matched popular expectations of the Messiah. But most important, he explained that the Son of man would rise again from the grave and return in glorious victory over evil.

In the Gospel of John. John's Gospel teaches the same message about the person of Jesus as the other Gospels, but uses an entirely different vocabulary. John speaks of Jesus in the opening chapter as the Word, a part of God himself. Throughout this Gospel, Jesus speaks of himself as the "Son" and refers to God as the "Father." There is clearly a distinction between the two; for example, the Son prays to the Father. Yet the relationship between the Father and the Son goes far beyond the relationship other people have with God. Jesus' relationship with the Father was unique. In one debate with the Jews, Jesus actually used the title "I am"—the very name of God—in reference to himself. Because of that claim, the Jews tried to kill him for blasphemy. (Eventually, of course, they succeeded.) This complexity in the character of Jesus places us under obligation to study the Gospel records carefully. Jesus was a *man* born among men, and at the same time he was *God* present with men.

Because the Father had revealed himself through the Son, the believer can enjoy abundant life. The Jews believed that there would be a new kind of life which would be unique to the so-called age to come. But John's Gospel promises that life in this present age. John did not mean merely that believers could understand God or know about God. He meant that they could know God himself through his Son. They could enter into a relationship with God. So in John's Gospel Jesus is portrayed as God's ultimate self-revelation. He demands faith in himself as the entrance into eternal life.

In the letters of Paul. In the past hundred years or so, a few scholars have tried to convince their readers that the Gospels convey the religion *of* Jesus while Paul invented a religion *about* Jesus. Nothing could be farther from the truth. The Gospel writers were just as theological as Paul. Everything in the New Testament is an attempt to understand the theological significance of God's becoming man in Jesus of Nazareth. The Gospel writers used one literary form; Paul used another. Taken singly or together they communicate a consistent, whole picture.

Paul began, just as the Gospel writers did, by assuming the Old Testament picture of God. His concept of the individual as sinner, for example, is derived from that source. But his presentation of it was more rigorous than any of the Old Testament writers. As a result, his picture of humanity is much more pessimistic. Paul, however, did not draw the picture. He merely organized materials from the Old Testament. Paul insists that we must deal with people as they are, utterly defiled, not as we might like them to be. If human beings could choose to obey the Law, the problem might be somewhat simpler. But Paul insists (and he quotes extensively from the Old Testament to prove his point) that each individual human being is bound by sin. No one can choose to be obedient to the Law. The Law, if anything, incites people to disobedience!

But God, according to Paul, once again took the initiative, just as he had throughout the Old Testament. This time, however, his action was unique and remains so. He entered time and space to become a man. By so doing he brought salvation to man. For Paul, just as for John, Jesus is the eternal Son come in the flesh. The death of Christ is the event which broke the power of sin and death. And the resurrection of Jesus assures us that those who trust in him will also rise from the grave.

During the period between the Testaments the Jews moved increasingly toward the view that salvation depends upon obedience to the Law. Paul argued that this point of view totally misunderstands the core of Old Testament theology. God offered Israel a covenant at Sinai. That covenant both created a relationship between Israel and God and placed Israel under certain obligations. But nowhere in the Old Testament is it said that Israel received the covenant *because* she had obeyed the Law. In a similar way, God now offers forgiveness to each person. When God is reconciled to a person, that person must immediately accept certain responsibilities—both to God and to neighbors. But reconciliation is not gained through fulfilling those responsibilities. Reconciliation is God's free offer. Faith accepts that offer and participates in the reconciliation. The ability to fulfill God's demands follows as the natural (literally, the supernatural) result of the presence of the Spirit in those who believe.

People who accept forgiveness are reconciled with God. On a corporate level, they become part of the body of Christ, the church. This is one of Paul's most distinctive ideas. People are responsible to put their salvation into practice. They must learn new lifestyles, which are consistent with their new relationship with God. But the corporate aspects of salvation are also important. Each person is placed by God into the body of Christ, and that means that his or her growth toward full Christian maturity is linked to the growth of other members of that body. People are responsible to nurture other members of the body; conversely they are required by God to allow others to help them grow toward maturity. According to Paul, Christians cannot grow to maturity in isolation. Hence, Paul laid the foundation

for the early church as a nurturing, helping community of
believers.

Where to Begin
In conclusion, I would again like to suggest several biblical
books for you to read. Try beginning with Luke and Acts. These
two books will give you a feel for the life of Jesus and the development of the early church. Then read Paul's letter to the Romans. I must admit that Romans is difficult, but it will repay your
efforts. If you understand only a part of what you read the first
time through, do not worry. What you do understand will be
worth the effort. Next read 1 Corinthians, one of several letters
in which Paul discusses the concept of the body of Christ.

Finally, read John's Gospel for another viewpoint on the life
of Christ. These books will introduce you to three major writers
in the New Testament and three distinct kinds of literature. You
should enjoy them all, and they will undoubtedly add to your
understanding of the evangelical community.

Further Reading

Barker, Glenn W.; Lane, William L.; and Michaels, J. Ramsey. *The New
Testament Speaks*. New York: Harper & Row, 1969. An evangelical textbook on
the background and literature of the New Testament.

Bruce, F. F. *The New Testament Documents: Are They Reliable?* 5th ed., Downers
Grove, Ill.: InterVarsity Press, 1960. A defense of the accuracy and reliability
of the New Testament.

——————. *New Testament History*. Garden City, New York: Doubleday,
1972. A thorough Jewish history from the intertestamental period to about the
end of the first century.

Guthrie, Donald. *Jesus the Messiah: An Illustrated Life of Christ*. Grand Rapids:
Zondervan, 1972. An excellent, clear exposition written for the layman.

Hunter, A. M. *The Message of the New Testament*. Philadelphia: Westminster,
1944. A short survey of the theology of the New Testament.

Longenecker, Richard N. *The Ministry and Message of Paul*. Grand Rapids:
Zondervan, 1971. A short survey of the life of Paul. The last two chapters discuss Paul's thought and its relevance.

Stott, John R. W. *Basic Introduction to the New Testament*. Grand Rapids: Eerdmans, n.d. A brief survey of the New Testament summarizing the distinct
messages of the various authors.

THE FAITH
OF OUR
FATHERS

PART II

GROWING PAINS: THE EARLY CHURCH

6

Evangelical Christians in the United States tend to ignore the history of the church prior to 1517, the year that Martin Luther nailed his ninety-five theses on the church door in Wittenberg, Germany, and set the Reformation spinning. The church, some Protestants feel, accomplished little of note and did much to be regretted prior to Luther. Thus many evangelicals might be able to identify Protestant notables like Martin Luther, John Calvin, John Wesley and maybe even Jacob Arminius. But few would recognize equally important names from the early centuries or the medieval period, such as Athanasius, Anselm, Innocent III or Dominic.

This is very unfortunate. During the fifteen hundred years prior to the time of Luther, the church made decisions which have given form to its life and worship ever since. Evangelicalism is, therefore, firmly rooted in early and medieval Christianity.

This chapter looks at the first fifteen hundred years of the church's history. Obviously no one can survey such a lengthy period of time in so few pages. So instead I will focus on a few selected points at which the church made specific decisions which influence the way we understand or practice the Christian faith today. This should help us to appreciate the Catholic roots of evangelical Christianity.

From Persecuted Minority to State Religion

Toward the end of the first century, the church was faced with a vicious dilemma. Within the Roman empire only a few religious groups had been granted freedom of worship, and Christianity was not among the select number. Consequently, to participate in a Christian worship service was strictly illegal. The worshiper was liable to severe civil penalties.

Under the circumstances the church prudently met and worshiped in secret. But that very secrecy caused further problems. Rumor had it that Christians ate the body and blood of Jesus Christ during their worship services, so they were accused of cannibalism. Christians also referred to the church as the "bride of Christ," and outsiders wondered what kind of an initiation rite that entailed. But worst of all, most Christians refused to offer incense to the emperor. They were quite willing to affirm their loyalty to the state, but they insisted that an offering to the emperor would be idolatrous. To the Romans, for whom offering incense was something like our singing the national anthem, Christian stubbornness over such a trivial thing smacked of subversion. Consequently, the threat of persecution hung over Christians for almost three hundred years.

Contrary to the impression sometimes given, however, persecution was not continual. During short periods of intense persecution, confessing the Christian faith might bring martyrdom. Many early Christians were thrown to the lions or burned on crosses to entertain the Roman populace. But in truth the periods of intense persecution were rare, and Christians were left undisturbed for years at a time. Yet the threat remained until Emperor Constantine entered the scene.

Constantine was declared emperor of Rome by his troops following the death of his father in A.D. 306. But he had to fight for undisputed control over the empire. In 312, while he was preparing his troops for battle in Italy against Maxentius, he had a vision which turned him to the Christian faith. For the first time in history, the emperor of Rome was sympathetic to the church, and the significance of this can hardly be over-emphasized. The following year complete religious toleration was established throughout the empire at a meeting between Constantine and Licinius, the ruler of the eastern half of the realm. After three hundred years, Christianity was accepted— even respected—by the state. Subsequently, many government officials found it expedient to follow the emperor into the church, and the decision of the church to accept this influx of nominal Christians diluted the moral force of Christianity. Nonetheless, the legalization of Christianity enabled the church to participate directly in the shaping of Western culture during the next thousand years.

Community of Saints or School for Sinners?
From its inception, the church encouraged, even demanded, that Christians strive to be like Christ. Those who did not take the ethical values of the church seriously were excluded from the community (1 Corinthians 5). Given the rampant immorality of Roman society and the persecution of believers, it should come as no surprise that sexual immorality and apostasy (turning away from the faith) were the two sins which most frequently occupied the attention of the church after the first century.

The church took the stance very early that baptism, which could be administered only once, washed away all sins. Hence, one who was excluded from the community for postbaptismal sin could not be readmitted. There was no such thing as a "re-washing." Because of the harshness of that position, a second-century writer named Hermas argued that Christians could be forgiven once (but only once) after baptism for grave sins. This did not include the deadly sins of murder, adultery and apostasy. Clearly the church at this time was having trouble reconciling its image as a disciplined community with its image as a forgiving community. Was the church to be a community of saints or a school for sinners?

In the next century, after the church had amassed more pastoral experience in dealing with sinful members, Callistus, bishop of Rome (217-22), ruled officially that sincere penitents might be restored to Christian fellowship no matter how serious the crimes. The readmittance of the penitents depended solely on the sincerity of their repentance, not upon the gravity of the crimes. That ruling was, however, strenuously resisted by some who believed that the church was becoming morally lax.

The problem came to a head as a result of persecution under Emperors Decius (250-51) and Diocletian (303-05). After each of these two periods of persecution, the church decided that those who had denied the faith under the threat of death could be returned to fellowship if they were truly penitent. But in both instances, the ensuing conflict produced schism within the church. The followers of Novatian, who took the "rigorist" position, broke away from the church following the Decian persecution. About fifty years later the Donatists withdrew as a result of the church's leniency after the persecution under Diocletian. In spite of these defections, the church remained true to its commitment—its community was to include all those who were truly penitent.

Over the centuries the church gradually worked out a theology of penance. But in spite of a great deal of theological thought, the issue was not truly resolved—as far as Protestants are concerned—until the time of the Reformation.

Developing Church Structures

In describing the early church, we get the impression that it was a fairly united organization. That is only partially true. By the end of the first century, the church was still a loosely knit fellowship of individual churches which met in homes and elected men to serve in the role of priest/bishop. (The two words were interchangeable until about A.D. 100). But that loose organization soon caused problems. Someone had to take responsibility for ascertaining whether or not the doctrine of the apostles was being taught consistently in each local congregation.

Ignatius, a bishop from Antioch who wrote at the beginning of the second century, argued strenuously that the bishop must be "monarchical." Only an authoritative office in the church, he claimed, could guarantee purity of doctrine. Historical sources for the period are scanty, but Ignatius seems to have convinced the church. In any case, his position had become the norm by the end of the second century. The church moved toward a more fixed, hierarchical structure. Local churches continued to have deacons and priests, but after the second century an elected bishop would supervise a cluster of churches within a specified area. In subsequent centuries the church created the office of the archbishop in order to govern a larger area and to maintain control over local bishops. And eventually the bishop of Rome came to be called the "pope" and began to function as the head of the church in the West. Likewise the church in the East came to accept spiritual council and guidance from the "patriarch" of Constantinople. (These leaders are presumed to inherit their authority from the apostles.) Hierarchical church structure is hotly debated within the Protestant church today. Protestants deny the authority of the pope, but are divided over whether or not bishops have a legitimate place within the church.

The Search for Doctrinal Unity

Some of the decisions made in the early years of the church have subsequently been repudiated. But in one area, the early church was eminently successful in reaching a lasting consensus. The formulations of the doctrines of God and of Christ achieved by the church during those early centuries have united virtually all Christians since that time.

The value of theology. Before we launch into a discussion of those two doctrines, however, a preliminary question demands its moment. It is no secret that many Christians are uneasy about the whole theological enterprise. Is it, then, necessary for the church to confess her faith with theological rigor? Is the abstract theological enterprise really meaningful? Yes.

Everyone—Christian and non-Christian alike—has a theology of sorts. Each person holds (implicitly or explicitly) a system of beliefs about God, man and the world. No one ever has the luxury of deciding whether or not to have a theology. Hence the question for Christians must always be, Is my theology adequate? Can it be held and applied consistently? Christian theology is the attempt to articulate the Christian faith carefully. Theological work is intended to test personal theology by the Word of God. The value of that endeavor is surely beyond attack. It is true that Christian theologians have at times asked some relatively unimportant questions. But that does not justify denying the importance of the whole enterprise. A theology that discusses those issues which are clearly rooted in the Scriptures definitely has value for the church.

The second justification of the theological enterprise is historical. The church's theology has usually been a careful response either to false teaching within the church or to philosophies outside of the church which masquerade as Christianity. The church, quite obviously, cannot tolerate false teachings which are destructive of the faith. The proper response to bad theology is good theology. And that is the route that the church chose to take.

The doctrine of God. During the first two centuries, the church moved, in the main, to exclude theological concepts which were recognized as incompatible with authentic Christianity. But during the third and at the beginning of the fourth century, the church found herself divided over the precise nature of God. No one questioned the doctrine of the unity and uniqueness of God. That was an essential part of the church's Jewish heritage. Yet when Christians confessed that Jesus Christ was God's Son, they seemed to endanger that doctrine. The problem, therefore, was to articulate monotheism in a distinctly Christian form.

Modalism, one of the first suggested solutions to the problem, emphasized God's unity. The advocates of this position claimed that God reveals himself to us in three distinct ways or modes. But, they claimed, God is three only within our experience, from our perspective. God is not eternally three. The modes which we perceive are only the modes of his self-revelation. This solution did not commend itself to the church, and it was officially condemned. The New Testament clearly indicates that the Son of God existed and acted prior to his becoming a man. John, for example, wrote, "In the beginning was the Word, and the Word was with God" (1:1).

A second attempt to solve the problem is associated with a presbyter from Alexandria named Arius. He argued that since the Father "begat" the Son, the Son must be a part of the created order. The Son may be the first of all creation, and he may have an absolute pre-eminence; God may have created the world through the Son; but the Son is a created being distinct from the Father. Arius's theology was persuasive, and many chose to accept his theological solution to the problem of the nature of God. Others, including the bishop of Alexandria and one of his deacons named Athanasius, were adamantly opposed. Arius's theology threatened to split the church.

Emperor Constantine ignored the whole problem until it became clear that the breach would not heal without some help. He called a council of bishops which met in the city of Nicaea in 325. Their task was to hammer out a solution to the issue once and for all—to find a way of affirming the deity of Christ without denying the unity of God. Under the leadership of Athanasius, the council concluded that Arius's solution was unsatisfactory. If the Son of God is a part of the created order, then the church's worship of him is idolatrous. And if the Son is not God, then he cannot be the self-revelation of God. Finally, if Christ is not God, he cannot have accomplished the redemption of the human race.

After a period of debate, the council reached agreement on how to articulate what has since been known as "trinitarian monotheism." The council declared that God is indeed one, but not simply one. His very being is complex in three distinct ways. He is throughout eternity the Father, Son and Holy Spirit. The word *trinity* which came out of those discussions is not a biblical word. It is rather an invented word which tries to guard both the unity of God and also his complexity. The theological formulation which they produced did *not explain* God. It laid the foundation for the Nicene Creed, which was written about fifty years later. That Creed has helped the church guard the doctrine of God since that time by affirming clearly both the unity and the threefold complexity of God's nature.

The doctrine of Christ. The second major doctrinal dispute faced by the early church concerned the nature of Christ. The Council of Nicaea had affirmed that Jesus Christ was indeed God himself. It did not deal with the question, How is it possible for God and man to be joined in one being? There were two distinct approaches to the problem, associated with Alexandria and Antioch. The Alexandrians began with the concept of the Logos, the Word of God, and tried to explain how the Logos became man. The Antiochenes began at the opposite pole. They assumed that Jesus was a man and tried to explain how his humanity could have been taken into the Godhead.

Apollinarius, a defender of the Alexandrian approach, insisted that human flesh is always united with human spirit in a living relationship. In Jesus Christ, however, human flesh is united to and given life by the eternal Logos. Thus the Logos took up human flesh in the Incarnation in order to live as a man. The church, however, quickly saw that the solution of Apollinarius would not do. Our soul or spirit is an essential element of our humanity. Human nature is more than just fleshly existence. If Jesus did not have a human spirit, but had the divine Logos instead, then he lacked that which is most distinctive of our humanity. By this theory, God did not really become *man* at all.

An Antiochene approach to the problem became the focus of controversy when Nestorius, the patriarch of Constantinople, was asked to settle an argument over whether or not Mary could be called the "God-bearer," a title widely used in Alexandrian circles. He ruled that Mary should properly be called the "Christ-bearer." He pointed out that humanity is tempted, suffers and grows. God, in contrast, cannot share those experiences. Therefore, the two natures of Christ must be held distinct. God and man were indeed *conjoined* in Christ, but not mixed. The opponents of Nestorius, however, thought that he was teaching that Christ was in some sense "bipersonal," that the human Jesus and the divine Word were merely united morally, but not united in their being. Indeed, some of the followers of Nestorius taught just that. The whole issue got terribly muddled because of political and personality conflicts. It is difficult to straighten out the details. We know, however, that the point of view attributed to Nestorius was condemned at the Council of Ephesus in 431 on the ground that such a point of view would destroy the personal unity of the Christ.

The Council of Ephesus, however, was far from being a model of Christian decorum and openness. Some participants refused afterward to accept its conclusions. These Nestorian Christians subsequently separated themselves from the majority of the church and formed a separate church centered in the area of Persia. During the following centuries, the Nestorians became active missionaries toward the East (they actually established the Christian faith in China in the seventh and eighth centuries), and thus they made an important contribution to the expansion of Christianity. They were eventually decimated by persecution, but even today small pockets of Nestorian Christians survive in Iraq and Iran.

A monk named Eutyches suggested yet another way to explain how God became man. Eutyches was horrified by the Antiochene approach. In reaction he taught that in Christ a full and complete human nature had been taken up entirely into the divine nature. Only one nature remained afterward. Even the body of our Lord became a divine body. Eutyches' one-sided solution could not, rather obviously, account for Jesus' humanity. Some people even wondered if he were in fact a Docetist. (The Docetists were Christians who adopted the Greek, Gnostic belief that the physical world is evil. They argued that the Son of God could not actually have taken on human flesh because this would have contaminated him. Therefore, Christ merely *appeared* to have become a man.) But Eutyches accomplished one thing. His theology was the final straw which forced the church to clarify the Christological issue.

A council was held in Chalcedon in 451, and each of the three points of view just surveyed was considered and condemned. In a positive statement the church affirmed aspects of both the Antiochene and the Alexandrian points of view. Christ did indeed have *two natures;* that is, he was both truly God and truly man. But he was only *one person.* The union did not join God and *a* man. It united, without blending, the divine nature and human nature in one person. In the Incarnation the eternal Son of God took upon himself all that is truly human. He took up our human nature, all of it, but not a distinct human personality.

Again, some participants dissented vigorously. After the council these dissenters, most of whom were from the Alexandrian tradition, refused to accept the Chalcedonian settlement. They insisted that the humanity of Christ had been taken into his deity so that there remained *only one nature* after the union. In the ensuing centuries the issue came up again and again, but the church as a whole continued to hold to the Chalcedonian settlement. The dissenters, known as Monophysite Christians, eventually broke away from the mainstream. Their descendants (the Coptic Church in Egypt is the most famous example) continue to teach their distinctive approach to Christology to the present day.

These decisions regarding the nature of God and of Christ are among the most significant ones made by the church during those early centuries. They definitely influence the way in which contemporary evangelicals read their Bibles. At the same time it is important for evangelicals to remember that some people who confess the name of Christ have separated themselves over how

Jesus' precise nature is to be defined.

Evangelicals today still use the ancient creeds to articulate basic Christian doctrines. Both the Nicene Creed (a more elaborate statement than the one formulated at the Council of Nicaea) and the Apostles' Creed (which first appeared around A.D. 340) have been used frequently throughout the history of the church.

The Nicene Creed

I believe in one God the Father Almighty, Maker of heaven and earth, And of all things visible and invisible:

And in one Lord Jesus Christ, the only-begotten Son of God; Begotten of his Father before all worlds, God of God, Light of Light, Very God of very God; Begotten, not made; Being of one substance with the Father; By whom all things were made; Who for us men and for our salvation came down from heaven, And was incarnate by the Holy Ghost of the Virgin Mary, And was made man: And was crucified also for us under Pontius Pilate; He suffered and was buried: And the third day he rose again according to the Scriptures: And ascended into heaven, And sitteth on the right hand of the Father: And he shall come again, with glory, to judge both the quick and the dead; Whose kingdom shall have no end.

And I believe in the Holy Ghost, The Lord, and Giver of Life, Who proceedeth from the Father and the Son; *Who with the Father and the Son together is worshipped and glorified; Who spake by the Prophets: And I believe one Catholic and Apostolic Church: I acknowledge one Baptism for the remission of sins; And I look for the Resurrection of the dead: And the Life of the world to come. Amen.*

The Apostles' Creed

I believe in God the Father Almighty, Maker of heaven and earth:

And in Jesus Christ his only Son our Lord: Who was conceived by the Holy Ghost, Born of the Virgin Mary: Suffered under Pontius Pilate, Was crucified, dead, and buried: He descended into hell; The third day he rose again from the dead: He ascended into heaven, And sitteth on the right hand of God the Father Almighty: From thence he shall come to judge the quick and the dead.

I believe in the Holy Ghost: The holy Catholic Church; The Communion of Saints: The Forgiveness of sins: The Resurrection of the body: And the Life everlasting. Amen.

Monasticism: The Fight against Worldliness

For a variety of reasons Protestants have tended to view monasticism as misdirected at best and possibly even unchristian. Nonetheless, it deserves brief attention in a book which focuses on evangelical Christianity for two reasons. First of all, the monks were the major missionary arm of the church during the medieval period. Europe was won to Christianity largely through their efforts, a fact which may come as a surprise. Thus, the monks are an important link in the chain of witnesses through whom the message of Jesus Christ was passed down to us. Second, monasticism must be examined at least briefly in order to grasp the significance of Luther's rebellion against his own monastic vows during the Reformation.

The origin of monasticism. During the third century, the church was becoming increasingly lax morally. In response, a small but steady stream of Christians began to drop out of society altogether in order to practice the Christian life as hermits. By choosing such a life, these dedicated Christians hoped to pursue holiness in a way which no longer seemed possible for those who lived within society and participated in the institutional church.

Anthony, an Egyptian who retreated into the desert toward the end of the third century, became so famous for his piety and spiritual wisdom that others began to congregate around him for spiritual advice and leadership. Out of this spontaneous movement came the first form of Christian monasticism, an unstructured association of hermits who lived in close proximity to each other. These "anchorites" (the proper term for ascetics who choose to withdraw from society to pursue holiness of life as hermits) practiced great austerity in order to subdue the flesh, devote themselves to prayer and battle against the demonic forces of Satan.

A generation later an Egyptian anchorite named Pachomius (287-346) brought about a decisive change in the complexion of monasticism by writing a "rule" designed to create a community where there had previously been only an association of hermits. Each monastery organized according to this new format was to be an economically self-sufficient unit. Each member of such a community devoted himself to the physical duties necessary for maintenance of the community, to instruction in and memorizing of the Scriptures, and to participation in the daily offices (worship services) and the weekly Eucharistic service.

Benedictine monasticism. Over the next two centuries, monasticism also began to flourish in the West. But many who chose the monastic way found it necessary to rewrite and adapt the original rules to their new context. Benedict of Nursia was one of many who participated in the process of creating a distinctly Western variety of monasticism. His ideas, however, displayed such balance and spiritual wisdom that they gradually displaced all rivals. Eventually Western monasticism came to be called Benedictine.

The friars. At the beginning of the thirteenth century, after a thousand years of monasticism, yet another form was born: the friars, or the mendicant orders. Prior to this time, monks had cloistered themselves in order to search for their own salvation and to pray for the needs of society at large. In contrast to this, the friars moved into society and into the new growing cities, in order to serve society in a more direct way.

Francis of Assisi, one of the most famous Christians of the medieval period, had a vision of God in 1209 after which he gave away his wealth and devoted himself to a life of preaching and service to the needy. His example struck those around him with such force that he soon had a growing band of followers. After only a few years, the Order of Friars Minor (or Franciscans) received the approval of Pope Innocent III.

A few years later a Spanish cleric named Dominic formed an order which was devoted to preaching, scholarship and the intellectual defense of the Christian faith. The new Dominican order, called the "Order of Preachers," eventually produced Thomas Aquinas, probably the most influential theologian of the period.

The Growth of the Papacy

During the medieval period, the structure of the institutional church was altered in two distinct ways. The first of these was that the status and influence of the papal office rose in importance, thus setting the stage for Luther's rebellion against Rome.

Toward the end of his reign (330), Constantine moved the administrative center of the empire from Rome to Constantinople, a city which he had built on the European side of the Bosporus straits. He did so in order to locate the administrative center of the empire closer to its geographical center. As an unintentional by-product of that move, the bishop of Rome was able to maintain more independence than the Eastern patriarchs. By the eighth century the pope was recognized as both a political lord and the most influential bishop in the Western church. About this same time archbishops throughout the European continent began to recognize the importance of gaining papal approval for their appointments.

After a period of decline in the tenth century, the status and responsibilities of the pope steadily and rapidly increased. Pope Gregory VII (1073-85), for example, steadfastly refused to admit that a layman—even the emperor himself—could appoint bishops. That right, he insisted, belonged to the papacy. In fact, he excommunicated Emperor Henry IV in defense of it. The actual *power* of the papacy reached its peak in the reign of Innocent III (1198-1216), but the summit of papal *claims* was not reached until a hundred years later. In his bull *Unam sanctam,* Boniface VIII (1294-1303) declared that it is absolutely necessary to be subject to the Roman pope in order to receive salvation. The very necessity of making such a pronouncement, however, was in itself indicative of problems. Beginning at about that time the papacy went into decline.

The Church Divides

The second major change in the church during medieval times was its division into two distinct institutions. The final separation of the Orthodox tradition of the East from the Catholic tradition of the West is usually dated in 1054. This was, however, the culmination of a gradual trend which occurred over several hundred years. From its origin, the Roman empire had been divided into a Greek-speaking East and a Latin-speaking West with corresponding cultural differences. The church quite naturally reflected these divergencies. This cultural contrast within the church grew, however, and became a cause of friction during the early part of the medieval period. None of the particular issues alone was very important, but each widened the breach. The formula for fixing the proper day to celebrate Easter, for example, was different in the two traditions. This caused problems during the second and third centuries.

During the eighth century churches from the two traditions had a relatively brief, but intense, argument about a more theological issue: Were icons, the images used in the churches as a part of worship, appropriate or not? Although it took over a generation to settle the issue, the details of the feud need not detain us here. But the aftershocks of this disagreement are worth noting. As a result of this conflict, the pope turned away from the old Greco-Roman world and sought a closer political relationship with the new Germanic powers to the north. The shift appeared minor at the time, but it was a portent of the ultimate religious separation to come.

Between the eighth century and the early years of the eleventh century, the Western church gradually accepted an addition to the Nicene Creed. The word *filioque,* which means "and the Son," was added to it in the West in order to affirm that the Spirit proceeds from *both* the Father and the Son (see p. 91). The Eastern churches protested that the word was an innovation, while the Western churches affirmed that the idea was theologically sound. Had it not been for centuries of bickering, the dispute probably could have been resolved. Under the circumstances it helped to drive the wedge deeper.

During the eleventh century a breach developed between the pope in Rome and the patriarch in Constantinople over who should have religious jurisdiction over southern Italy. Then, in 1054, representatives of the pope excommunicated the patriarch; the patriarch reciprocated! Observers at that time did not consider the breach terribly important. It proved, nonetheless, to be a sore which never healed. After that time the Western churches, which followed the pope in Rome, developed the distinct "Catholic tradition." The Eastern churches, by following the patriarch in Constantinople and denying the authority of the pope, developed an independent "Orthodox tradition." To this day, the breach has not been healed. Since American evangelicalism has its roots in the Western tradition, we will limit our study to its development.

Scholasticism: Between Faith and Reason

The eleventh century saw yet another striking development: a great surge of intellectual energy, since known as scholasticism, passed through the church in the West. Within theological circles discussion focused particularly on the relationship between faith and reason. Are the two compatible or contradictory? If they are compatible, how should Christian theologians go about their work? Should they begin with faith and only use reason to enhance it? Or can they begin with reason and progress logically toward faith? Can reason, for example, demonstrate logically that what the Church believes and teaches is true? The early scholastics answered this last question with an unequivocal yes. Anselm of Canterbury, for example, wrote a book entitled *Cur Deus Homo (Why God Became Man)* in which he tried to demonstrate that the Incarnation was a rational necessity. He reasoned that it was the only way in which God could deal with the problem of sin created by the Fall.

In the thirteenth century further intellectual progress was made when the works of the Greek philosopher Aristotle were translated into Latin for the first time and introduced into European universities. Most of Aristotle's writings had been lost to Europe during the course of the Middle Ages, even though they were preserved and studied in Arabic centers of learning. This reintroduction of Aristotle's works created a theological problem of the first magnitude. The commentaries on Aristotle then available were written by some of the greatest Islamic philosophers. As these secondary works began to circulate along with Aristotle's, they had a profound impact on the university students, some of whom became convinced of unorthodox ideas. For a while the Church tried to censor the whole subject. But in the middle of the thirteenth century the challenge of Aristotle was picked up by Thomas Aquinas, who tried to write a theology which would take Aristotle's philosophy into account. *Summa Theologica* and *Summa contra Gentiles,* his two large multivolume works which were the results, remain as the high-water mark of the scholastic enterprise.

Scholasticism degenerated between 1300 and 1500. The intellectual movement which had begun by trying to show that faith is indeed rational ended in frustration. Many important thinkers concluded that while faith is not irrational, it cannot be completely demonstrated in a logically convincing way.

Systematizing the Sacraments

During the same period of time, the theology of the sacraments was elaborated, clarified and systematized. This "sacramental system" provides the classic Catholic answer to the question, How can I be saved?

According to medieval Catholic theology, God conveys his grace to men and women by means of the sacraments, the special rites which are guarded, practiced and explained by the Church. Just which of the Church's many rites were, in reality, sacramental (that is, grace endowing), had been much debated throughout the centuries. Then, during the fifteenth century the number was officially and finally fixed at seven: baptism, confirmation, penance, the Eucharist or the Mass, marriage, ordination and extreme unction. Four of these demand special attention here because of their significance for the development of contemporary evangelical theology.

Baptism. As understood by the Church since the early second century, baptism bestows the grace which washes away the taint of original sin (the fallen nature we inherit because of Adam's sin) and conveys salvation. Without it, everyone would face damnation. Each person is tainted with original sin and therefore cannot hope to enter heaven. Baptism guarantees that individuals, so long as they do not fall into certain so-called deadly sins, will eventually attain eternal life. Baptism, however, does not guarantee that one would go *directly* to heaven. For many people additional cleansing would be necessary after death in a place called *purgatory,* but as long as one avoided the deadly sins hell was not a danger.

Penance. The scholastics developed a more systematic and thorough understanding of the sacrament of *penance* in order to enable the Church to further deal with the problem of sin. The Church concluded that an act of penance consists of several parts: confession, contrition (sorrow about sin), satisfaction (a meritorious work done by the penitent to render compensation for the sin), and absolution (declaration by the priest that the sin is forgiven). When properly administered, believing Christians could find a very real aid to spiritual growth in this sacrament. Unfortunately, certain elements of the sacrament of penance were terribly abused during the closing centuries of the medieval period.

Three related doctrines, in particular, became the focus of intense controversy: merit, the treasury of merit and indulgences. Some claimed that the saints had done more than was necessary to insure that they would by-pass purgatory and enter heaven directly. The extra merits done by them during their lifetimes accumulated in a treasury of merit which was founded by the work of Christ and was at the disposal of the Church. So the pope, acting in the name of the Church, could for good reason transfer merit to others. Such transfers were effected by issuing indulgences. Those who went on crusades, for example, might receive total remission of sins on the basis of this treasury by means of an indulgence. During the fourteenth and fifteenth centuries, the requirements for remission of sins were gradually lowered. By the year 1500 forgiveness could be "bought" for an appropriate donation to the Church.

Mass. The Last Supper as instituted by Christ and recorded in the Gospels was a simple meal. Through the centuries, however, it developed into an elaborate celebration called the Eucharist or the Mass. The service, which was understood as a re-enactment of the sacrifice of Christ, culminated when the bread and wine were blessed by the priest and shared with the congregation. In partaking of these elements worshipers received grace which advanced them toward eternal life.

At the original supper, Jesus had said as he passed bread and wine to his disciples, "This is my body" and "This is my blood" (Mk. 14:22, 24; Lk. 22:19-20). Consequently, the Church had always taught that Christ is actually and literally present in the elements of the celebration. How he is present had not previously been clearly explained, but during the scholastic period the solution to that problem was worked out on the basis of the newly recovered Aristotelian philosophy. According to the Catholic doctrine of "transubstantiation," the outward form of the bread and wine (its color and texture, for example) remains unchanged, but the substance which stands beneath the visible elements becomes that of the body and blood of Christ.

Ordination. This sacrament completes the sacramental system. When a bishop lays hands on a man in the act of ordination, he bestows on that man the power to perform the sacraments. Consequently, except under extremely unusual circumstances, only a priest is allowed to baptize or to celebrate the Eucharist in a Catholic church. The grace of ordination can never be lost. Once that power is bestowed by a bishop, it cannot be retracted, even if the priest should fall into mortal sin. This is an essential link in the system because it guarantees that the spiritual state of a priest cannot affect the progress of an individual soul toward salvation. If a person was baptized by a properly ordained priest, then he or she indeed received the grace of salvation—even if the priest subsequently proved to be unworthy.

This concludes our whirlwind tour through the first 1500 years of church history. Although the account is incomplete, it lays a foundation for understanding the controversies that followed. The formation of the institutional church, the development of church doctrine, the growth of monasticism, the theology of the scholastics and the sacramental system all become sources of controversy during the Reformation.

Further Reading

Latourette, Kenneth Scott. *Christianity through the Ages.* New York: Harper & Row, 1965. A short, readable survey of the history of the church by one of America's most able historians.

Richardson, Alan. *Creeds in the Making: A Short Introduction to the History of Christian Doctrine.* New York: Macmillan, 1951. A well-written and stimulating discussion about Christian doctrine.

Knowles, David. *Christian Monasticism.* New York: McGraw-Hill, 1969. A richly illustrated, interesting history of the monastic movements from the earliest years to the present (covers only cloistered orders).

Gilson, Etienne. *Reason and Revelation in the Middle Ages.* New York: Scribners, 1938. A short, highly readable introduction to scholasticism.

RUMBLINGS
AND EARTHQUAKE:
THE REFORMATION

7

On October 31, 1517, Martin Luther, friar of the Augustinian Hermits, nailed to the door of the Castle Church in Wittenberg, Germany, an offer to debate "ninety-five theses on indulgences." That challenge, according to later interpretations, launched the Protestant Reformation. Luther and his associates aimed, at least initially, simply to reform the Roman Catholic Church. Instead, the Church was split, and the Protestant movement itself eventually divided into four distinct branches. In retrospect, Luther's challenge to debate stands as one of the decisive turning points in church history. Of course this momentous event of 1517 had its roots in the past. Some of these were examined in the previous chapter.

This period of history is not a pretty one; nonetheless, it is essential to look at it in order to understand Luther's actions. The description is not intended to be a polemic against the Catholic Church. Protestant and Catholic scholars disagree about many things, but not about the state of the Church at the time of Luther. Every student today recognizes that the Church of that period desperately needed to be reformed. Where Protestant and Catholic scholars differ is over the question of whether or not Luther's response to the situation was the correct one.

On the Eve of the Revolt

The state of the clergy. As indicated in the previous chapter, the sacramental system is, according to Catholic theology, the central element in the ongoing work of the Church. By the very nature of the sacrament of ordination, an individual priest could cease to uphold high priestly standards without doing essential damage to the life of the local congregation. He was only required to enact the sacramental rites of the Church regularly. Unfortunately, during this period priests who functioned at this minimal level were far from exceptional.

Educational standards among the clergy were also low. In Europe Latin had been the language of education and religion for centuries. Yet during the late medieval period the average priest would have been just barely literate in that language. And since Bibles were handcopied until about 1450, few priests owned their own. Understandably, few clergy possessed more than minimal knowledge about the Bible, and most lay people knew only a few of the more popular stories from Genesis or the Gospels.

Further, the standards for religious practice were often low during this period of church history. According to Catholic theology, the Mass was a meritorious work which would soften the penalties for lesser sins. Indeed, a priest could say Mass on behalf of one who had died in order to aid the progress of the deceased through purgatory and into heaven. In practice this meant that a wealthy person could endow a clerical position at a church or cathedral and thereby guarantee that masses would be said on his behalf in perpetuity. A priest who held such a position was required to say a certain number of masses daily on behalf of the original patron—whether or not anyone else was present. Not surprisingly, priests who held such positions often allowed these obligatory masses to degenerate into hurried, perfunctory rituals.

The moral level of the clergy in the century prior to the Reformation was even more bleak than the educational and religious levels. People commonly complained about drunkenness among the clergy, and priests often kept concubines. Before his break with Rome, Zwingli, one of the Reformers, wrote to the bishop on behalf of himself and several other priests who requested official permission to marry in order to legalize their present situations. The standards among the bishops and archbishops were no higher. In short, the state of the clergy at all levels was far from being exemplary of faith and practice. It was a deplorable situation.

The state of the institutional Church. The problems of the Church extended to more than just the personal life of the clergy. The Church as an institution had become an integral part of the feudal system during the course of the Middle Ages, and this fact had repercussions for the economic life of Europe. For example, over the centuries the Church had been given a good deal of land in Europe, and much of that land was income producing. Most clerical positions within the medieval Church were funded by income from a particular piece of land, which means that the one who filled such a position (a "benefice," as it was called) would be guaranteed a certain specified income. From one point of view, therefore, the right to hold a particular benefice could be viewed as a good investment. Thus, "simony," the purchase of benefices by those who desired income, became a problem. Officially the practice was condemned by the Church, but unofficially it was common at all levels. In short, the Church had conformed to the world. The concept of the cleric as landlord had displaced the concept of the pastor as shepherd of the flock.

The pope, the greatest landlord in Europe, was also thoroughly immersed in the system. In the early part of the fourteenth century, Pope Clement V moved the papacy to Avignon, a city on the border between France and Italy, because of the political instability of Rome at the time. He thus initiated what has been called the "Babylonian captivity" of the papacy. Because of financial pressures created by this move and because of the growth of the papal bureaucracy, successive popes became increasingly concerned with locating new sources of income for their office.

Simony was condemned because it was such an obvious evil, but it continued to be practiced. And other conventions arose which were more morally ambiguous. For example, the popes of the fourteenth century began leaving a vacated post empty for a period of time in order to collect the income it generated. From one point of view, the vacancy did not really matter. Pastoral care was normally handled by an assistant anyway. So the papal office might just as well collect the revenues as anyone else. Still, the practice of holding positions open did little to improve the quality of ministry within the Church. At the highest level, the pressing need to pay the bills had eclipsed the call to provide spiritual and moral leadership.

Efforts toward reform prior to Luther. During this period a variety of efforts to reform the Church were attempted, a fact which indicates that God was indeed at work within his church. In 1378 the cardinals attempted to depose a sitting pope (Urban VI), and they elected a new one (Clement VII). The result, however, was the Great Schism which went on for some forty years. The "Conciliar Movement," an attempt to deal with this specific problem, reached its apex at the Council of Constance in 1414. It was hoped that this council would be able to end the schism and to suggest reforms for the high Church offices. Unfortunately, however, successive popes were able to outmaneuver the council, and the movement gradually died.

Nevertheless, reform continued in certain areas because of the efforts of conscientious individuals. In England toward the end of the fourteenth century, John Wycliffe helped translate the Bible into English and encouraged the work of nonordained preachers. After his death, his followers, who became known as

"Lollards," continued to try to reform the English Church. Meanwhile, Wycliffe's writings traveled to the Continent where they influenced John Hus, a Bohemian preacher who was also interested in Church reform. His radical views alienated him from the Church, and he was eventually sentenced to death. But his followers in Bohemia continued to work for reform up to the time of Luther.

By the end of the fifteenth century the growth of nationalism and changes in the economic balance in Europe created an environment more conducive to reform. Such was the setting when Martin Luther nailed his challenge to debate on the church door in Wittenberg.

Luther and Lutheranism

In 1505, at the age of twenty-one, Martin Luther made a hasty decision to become a monk. He had been struck down by a bolt of lightning and in his fright had vowed to join an order. Two years later he was ordained to be a priest as well.

As he celebrated his first Mass, a service which was intended to assure him of God's forgiveness, Luther was overwhelmed with a sense of his own unworthiness. His search for God had only disclosed to him the immense distance between God's expectations and his achievements as a monk. Several years later, he was sent on a pilgrimage to Rome to transact business as a representative of his order. But what he witnessed there shook him to the core. He saw, for example, priests saying Mass hurriedly with little or no concern for its religious significance. The blatant moral hypocrisy shook him so much that he began to question the whole of the sacramental system.

After his return Luther pursued the degree of Doctor of Theology and completed it in 1512. Then for the next few years he studied and lectured on the Bible at the University of Wittenberg. Finally Luther discovered in the Bible the peace with God that had eluded him since he entered the monastery. In Romans he read of what he described as the "righteousness by which through grace and sheer mercy God justifies us through faith." Luther said he felt himself "to be reborn and to have gone through open doors into paradise." He found that peace came through faith in Jesus Christ, not through the accepted system of sacraments.

Although Luther's rediscovery of Paul's doctrine of justification by faith gave him the internal peace with God that he so desired, that doctrine was to disrupt the external peace of Western Christendom. During the century prior to the Reformation, the Roman Church had greatly elaborated its teachings concerning indulgences. By Luther's time the Church was teaching that acts of charity created merit for individuals and thus aided their progress toward complete salvation. But the Church defined *charity* very broadly. The concept included not only acts of compassion, but also the veneration of relics and contributions toward the Church's building programs.

While Luther had been struggling to find peace with God, Duke Frederick the Wise of Saxony, the founder of the university where Luther taught, had been amassing a large collection of relics in Wittenberg for the veneration of the faithful. In addition to housing this famous collection of relics, Wittenberg was an important destination for religious pilgrims. Each year on All Saints Day (November 1), a plenary indulgence was dispensed in the Castle Church. This was a special indulgence which granted the recipient remission from *all* sins. It was virtually inevitable that Luther's theological change would lead him into conflict with the established religious practices. But the adoration of relics in the Castle Church was not, as a matter of fact, the occasion for his attack on indulgences.

At the age of twenty-four, Albert of Brandenburg already held the sees of Halberstadt and Magdeburg. Despite his youth he hoped to be named archbishop of Mainz in addition, which would have made him primate of all of Germany. Albert knew that Pope Leo X was in need of funds, so in 1514 he offered a contribution large enough to overcome any problems which might stand in the way of his being named by the pope to yet another position. It was agreed that Albert would be named archbishop, and an indulgence would be promulgated in Germany. Half of the funds collected through the sale of these indulgences would go to Rome to build St. Peter's Basilica, and half would go to Albert to repay the rather large loan which he was forced to incur in order to gain the new position from the pope.

A Dominican friar named Tetzel was commissioned to sell this indulgence in the vicinity of Wittenberg in the fall of 1517. His pitch was crass at best. Who, he asked, would leave his mother in purgatory when for a mere sum of money she could be given eternal rest? At that juncture Luther decided that the time had come to pit his doctrine of justification against the accepted practices of the Church. On the day before All Saints Day, the most important festival of the Church year in Wittenberg, Luther posted his ninety-five theses on indulgences on the Castle Church door. By that act he declared his opposition to the commercialization of the relationship of the individual with God.

Luther intended his theses which were written in Latin, to be read only by Church theologians. They were soon translated into German, however, and distributed throughout the country. As a result the whole of Germany became involved in the controversy. Gradually the Church realized the depths of the protest and took steps to silence Luther. But Luther himself had gradually come to see the deeper implications of the biblical doctrine of justification. By 1520 he was willing to take on the whole Church, including the pope himself, in order to purge the Church of false doctrine. In contrast to previous reformers, Luther did not see immorality as the chief problem within the Church. That was merely symptomatic of the more fundamental problem—the Church's total misunderstanding of the way a person is set right with God. During that year Luther wrote three treatises which virtually precluded any future compromise. Even the peace-loving Erasmus declared the breach irreparable after reading the second of these "Reformation treatises."

About this time Emperor Charles V realized that the conflict was coming to have political overtones. Consequently, Luther was given a promise of safe conduct and ordered to appear before the parliament (or "Diet") of the Holy Roman Empire which was to meet the following year in Worms. Luther attended in spite of the obvious danger. At the meeting of the Diet Luther was asked to recant, but he refused since no effort had been made to refute his understanding of Scripture. Before the assembled German Diet, he insisted that Scripture, not the Church, must be the final authority for determining correct doctrine.

Shortly after that historic appearance, Luther was spirited out of town by order of Duke Frederick the Wise for his own protection and taken secretly to Wartburg castle, where he lived in exile for the next nine months. The forced retreat provided him with the opportunity to translate the Bible into German. Early in 1522 Luther decided to return to Wittenberg against the orders of the Duke. Henceforth, he was a criminal in the eyes of the empire and a heretic in the eyes of the Roman Catholic Church. In his own eyes and the eyes of his followers, he was a defender of the biblical truth that a person is justified by faith *alone*. By the end of the century, Lutheranism was firmly established in northern Germany and the Scandinavian countries, where it has remained the established state religion. Two hundred years later, when large numbers of Germans and Scandinavians emigrated to the United States, Luther's church crossed the Atlantic and became one of the major Protestant traditions here.

Zwingli, Calvin and the Reformed Tradition in Switzerland
Since all of sixteenth-century Europe was ripe for reform, it is not surprising to find that people of other countries joined with Luther. Huldreich Zwingli, the Reformer of Zurich, Switzerland, is less known than Luther. His influence is in evidence when Baptists and Brethren celebrate the Lord's Supper instead of the Eucharist or the Mass) as a memorial of Christ.

After receiving an excellent university education, Zwingli chose to enter the priesthood in 1506. Thereafter his ongoing study of Scripture led him to see that much of the life of the Church cried out for spiritual renewal. In obedience to God's Word he proclaimed from the pulpit the biblical perspective which he was coming to understand. His preaching differed from Luther's at one important point. All of Luther's preaching and reforming activities reflected his own personal discovery of the significance of justification by faith. Zwingli, in contrast, grew into his role as a Reformer more gradually. He was not grasped by one central idea which guided all of his work. Nonetheless, he was deeply convinced that all of life, including the life of the church, must be lived in obedience to Scripture. So when he was called in 1519 to become pastor of the Great Church in Zurich, he set about reforming it in a more piecemeal way. Each time he came to see that a particular aspect of life in Zurich was not in accord with the Bible, he would expound the biblical perspective on the issue from the pulpit. The Reform of the Church in Wittenberg was subordinated to Luther's concern to teach justification. The Reformation in Zurich expressed Zwingli's conviction that every aspect of Church life must conform to God's Word.

In time, Zwingli's ideas placed him in opposition to the Roman Catholic hierarchy, and he was asked by his superiors to bring his preaching and teaching more in line with traditional interpretations of the Bible. This he refused to do. In order to resolve the conflict between Zwingli's ideas and the traditional stance of the Church, the Zurich town council asked Zwingli to debate his ideas with a representative of the bishop of Constance. After the debate, held early in 1523, Zwingli was declared the winner by the council, and he was given formal permission to continue to preach reform. That act by the council was revolutionary. The Church claimed the right to determine the correct teaching of the Bible. Consequently the council's decision to support Zwingli instead of the official representatives of the Church at Rome was, in effect, a declaration that the church in Zurich was independent from both the Roman Catholic Church in general and from papal authority in particular.

By the end of the decade, it had become apparent that the Reformers and the Protestant princes needed to present a united front against the ardent Catholic Emperor Charles V. In particular they needed to reach a consensus on several theological issues which threatened to divide the young movement. Toward that goal, Philip of Hesse, one of the Protestant princes, arranged for Luther, Bucer (the leader of the reform movement in Strasbourg), Zwingli and several others to meet at his castle in Marburg, Germany, in October of 1529. During the course of the discussions, Luther and Zwingli agreed on all of the disputed points except one. They found it absolutely impossible to agree on the significance of the Lord's Supper. Their failure on that one issue had momentous implications. It demonstrated that Catholic fears were justified. The Protestant movement would not just split the Church; it would indeed fragment the body of Christ.

Zwingli died two years later while fighting alongside the Zurich militia against the Catholic cantons of Switzerland. Zwingli's reforming work was carried on in Zurich under the guidance of Heinrich Bullinger. But his real successor proved to be John Calvin, a brilliant young lawyer who was just then coming to a new understanding of the Christian faith.

Calvin was at that time studying at the University of Paris, where he associated with the reforming element. Through that association, he became acquainted with Luther's writings and eventually underwent a deeply felt conversion experience. Early in 1534 the political climate in France changed, and those who had publicly advocated reform were forced to flee from Paris. Calvin moved to Strasbourg and then on to Basel, Switzerland, where at the age of twenty-seven he published the *Institutes of the Christian Religion.* This work, revised five times during the course of his career, became the basic text of Reformed Protestantism.

Luther was never systematic in his theological work. Some of his writings addressed needed reforms in the Church, some responded to those who attacked his ideas, and some dealt with deviations within the Protestant movement itself. Calvin, in contrast, belonged to the second generation of the Reformation. By building on the mature work of both Luther and Zwingli, he was able to construct the first truly systematic expression of Protestant theology. In his work Calvin assumed the truth of Luther's doctrine of justification, but in his exposition of that doctrine he focused on the Augustinian concept of God's complete sovereignty in all human affairs—including personal salvation. No one, he insisted, deserves salvation. God, however, chooses sovereignly and graciously to rescue some from their justly deserved damnation.

After the first edition of the *Institutes* appeared in Basel, Calvin traveled into Italy. Later, as he passed through Geneva on his way to Strasbourg, the Reformer William Farel met him and demanded that he accept God's call to help with the Reform movement there. Calvin accepted the call and spent virtually all of the remainder of his life as the chief pastor and Reformer of the city of Geneva. Under Calvin's leadership, according to the Scottish Reformer John Knox, Geneva became "the most perfect school of Christ that ever was on earth since the days of the Apostles." Indeed, the city of Calvin was known throughout Protestant Europe as a city which encouraged a truly reformed Christian society.

In 1549 Calvin reached an agreement with Bullinger, Zwingli's successor in Zurich, which unified the Swiss Reformed tradition. In time that tradition influenced virtually every corner of Europe. Protestant exiles who fled England during the reign of the Catholic Queen Mary, studied with Calvin and after Mary's death returned to England with his ideas.

The Scots became Presbyterian through the efforts of John Knox, one of Calvin's students. The Reformers in France (called Huguenots) were greatly strengthened by the missionaries sent from the church in Geneva. Holland also became a center of Calvinist thought. And in time, the United States received and nurtured Calvin's ideas and the Reformed tradition from the Puritan, Presbyterian and Baptist immigrants.

The Evangelical Anabaptists

A third major Reformation group evolved in Zurich in opposition to the Zwinglian Reform. A small number of persons had begun to study the Scriptures with seriousness under Zwingli's guidance. By 1524, however, some of them had become impatient with the slow pace of reform and began disagreeing with his methods.

Zwingli was willing to work with the Zurich town council to bring about a gradual reform of the church. He assumed that it would take time to educate the populace so that they could appreciate the changes in the church which he planned to initiate. Zwingli did not want to push reform in the city faster than the people in general—or the council in particular—could bear. But Conrad Grebel, Georg Cajacob, Felix Manz and others began to question whether it was right to leave decisions regarding the reform of the church to the town council. Was it not imperative to reform the church in accord with the Word of God immediately—in opposition to the council if necessary?

This latent conflict between Zwingli and some of his followers came to a head when several preachers in the area around Zurich denied the legitimacy of infant baptism, refused to perform the rite and even preached against it. A debate was arranged on the topic by the town council. At that debate in January 1525, the council ruled that children should be baptized, and the dissidents were ordered to comply. Under pressure to choose, they met on the evening of January 21, 1525, and after much discussion and prayer, Conrad Grebel baptized Georg Cajacob. Henceforth, the group was known as the *Anabaptists,* which means "re-baptists," for Georg had been baptized as an infant. (The term *anabaptist* was later applied to a wide variety of sectarian groups which arose during this period, and this has caused a good deal of confusion. Consequently, most writers now refer to these particular men and their followers as Swiss Brethren or Evangelical Anabaptists in order to set them apart from some of the extremist groups included under the more general term.)

For a thousand years people had assumed that state and church should work together in order to create a Christian society. When the Evangelical Anabaptists denied government the right to enforce a uniform religious practice, they were persecuted as revolutionaries. Further, the Anabaptists encouraged opposition by their insistence that other forms of Protestantism were illegitimate.

By February of 1525 some Anabaptists had been jailed for their doctrine by the Protestant authorities in Zurich. Two years later, Felix Manz was drowned in Zurich for his refusal to forsake the Anabaptist persuasion. He was the first Protestant to be martyred by Protestants. At the Diet of Speier in 1529, Anabaptism was declared by Charles V to be a capital offense against the Holy Roman Empire. Deliberate steps were taken to exterminate the so-called heresy. These Reformers, in short, were hated, feared and persecuted by *both* Protestants and Catholics!

The Anabaptist movement survived in spite of persecution, but the struggles altered its character permanently. The aggressive missionary movement which threatened for a time to convert all of Europe, became defensive and turned inward on itself toward the end of the century. It has never regained the momentum that it had in those first years.

Yet the Anabaptist ideas live on. Freedom of religion, the revolutionary doctrine of the Evangelical Anabaptists, is now a legal right in the United States, along with the doctrine of the separation of church and state. Also, many groups today show themselves to be spiritual descendants of the original Anabaptists by practicing believer's baptism, accepting church discipline and commiting themselves to mutual care and concern.

Reformation in England

The English Reformation is the most complex of the four branches of the Protestant Reformation; yet it is probably the most significant for anyone who wishes to understand contemporary American evangelicalism. It is complex in that the Reformation in England began for political reasons and later was transformed into a religious phenomenon. It is significant because of the variety of churches it produced. In order to limit our scope somewhat, we will concentrate on the immediate cause of the English Reformation, the resolution of the Reformation crisis in England under the leadership of Queen Elizabeth, and the influence of the Church of England on the growth of evangelicalism in the United States.

Anticlericalism had always been an element in the British mentality, but it reached a peak in the early part of the sixteenth century. Church courts affected the laity in so many areas of life, and the monetary extractions of the Church were so heavy, that a broad cross section of the populace was ready to support changes in the religious situation. Soon after 1520 Luther's ideas began to seep into England. They met and joined forces with the native Lollard movement (the reform movement begun by John Wycliffe a century before).

At this time political pressures also came to bear on King Henry VIII. His Queen, Catherine of Aragon, was apparently not able to bear a male heir to the throne (although she gave birth to Princess Mary). Legally, there were precedents for a papal annulment, but under the circumstances that could hardly be granted. Catherine's nephew was Emperor Charles V of Germany, who at this time effectively controlled the papacy. Thus it would have been politically inexpedient for the pope to grant Henry the necessary dispensation. But from Henry's point of view, an annulment was a necessity. Dying without a male heir would expose England to possible anarchy in the battle over succession. To provide religious and legal grounds for his marriage to Anne Boleyn, Henry declared the English church independent from papal control and made himself head of the church. Thomas Cranmer, the newly appointed archbishop of Canterbury, granted the annulment.

This decision caused a three-way tug of war. Henry was determined to create an independent English church that would be Catholic, but not Roman Catholic. A conservative element, which included Princess Mary, hoped for reunion with Rome.

Finally a third group looked for a thorough reform of the church in England similar to that which was occurring in Germany and Switzerland. In the end the process of change which Henry loosed on England for personal and political reasons led to the creation of a new type of church.

After Henry's death in 1547 and the subsequent ascension of Edward VI, Henry's nine-year-old son by yet another marriage, the government came under the control of a Protestant regent who acted in the young king's place. During Edward's reign, the religious element of the English Reformation moved forward. English rather than Latin became the language of the liturgy and the Catholic doctrine of transubstantiation gave way to a Reformed understanding of the Eucharist. The prayer books written and published under Edward's authority expressed the new understanding.

But these changes were not yet permanent. Edward's death in 1553 allowed Mary, an ardent Catholic, to become Queen. She took immediate steps to re-establish the Catholic faith in England. If she had governed well, she might have been successful in her efforts. But her persecution of the Protestants was not thorough enough to decimate the movement; it merely aroused the people against both her and her policies. Many of the future leaders of England were strengthened in their Protestant understanding of the faith when they studied under Continental Reformers while in exile during Mary's reign. Her death after a reign of only five years ended Catholic hopes that England would rejoin the Roman Church. In retrospect, her reign appears as a brief period of reaction in an otherwise steady transition from English Catholicism to the Protestant Church of England.

After Queen Elizabeth took the crown in 1558, many of the Protestants who had chosen exile on the Continent during Mary's reign returned home. The more moderate of the "Marian Exiles" gained control of Parliament. Out of their interaction with Elizabeth over the form that the Church of England would take in the future came the Elizabethan Settlement of

1559. By that settlement, the Church of England would remain separate from Rome, the monarch was declared the supreme governor of the Church, and the worship services were conformed to a slightly revised edition of the 1552 prayer book written by Thomas Cranmer. Four years later, the doctrinal standards of the Church were expressed in the Thirty-nine Articles. As a result of these changes, the Church of England stood close to the Reformed tradition in doctrine, but somewhat nearer to the Roman Catholic Church in its form of worship.

The Church quickly developed several branches. In the decade after the settlement became law, a second wave of Marian Exiles returned to England. This group, which had spent the exile years in Geneva, returned with the vision of a Reformed church which would correspond fairly closely to the church in Calvin's Geneva. Hence they called upon the Church to continue its reforming work by removing all remnants of its Catholic past. But these "Puritans" were never able to alter permanently the original settlement.

Their descendants achieved this goal by another route. Some of them founded colonies in the New England area, and in so doing they created New England Congregationalism. Concomitantly, the Church of England itself took root as the Protestant Episcopal Church in the United States during the colonial period. Another group, similar in many ways to the Anabaptist groups on the Continent, chose to separate from the Puritans of the Church of England in order to form independent churches where believers would be baptized upon their confession of faith. Some of these early Baptists migrated to the United States, where they became the third branch of English Protestantism to take hold in American soil. Finally, the Evangelical Revival swept eighteenth-century England under the preaching of John Wesley and George Whitefield and brought the Methodist Church into existence both in England and the United States.

In sum, the whole spectrum of Protestant groups, those begun on the Continent as well as those from England, eventually developed in the United States. But the story of these various groups is less than half-told. What really matters for us is what they believed and taught. The next chapter will outline the theological achievements of those Reformation years.

Further Reading

Bainton, Roland H. *Here I Stand: A Life of Martin Luther.* New York: New American Library, 1951. The classic biography of Luther. Fascinating reading.

Bainton, Roland H. *The Reformation of the Sixteenth Century.* Boston: Beacon Press, 1956. An excellent, general introduction to the Reformation by one of America's leading scholars in the area.

Chadwick, Owen. *The Reformation.* New York: Penguin, 1964. An excellent, though somewhat dry, history of the Reformation.

Estep, William. *The Anabaptist Story.* Grand Rapids: Eerdmans, 1975. A short overview.

McNeill, John T. *The History and Character of Calvinism.* New York: Oxford Univ. Press, 1967. A solid study of Zwingli, Calvin and the Reformed branch of Protestantism by a well-known Calvin scholar.

Parker, T. M. *The English Reformation to 1558,* 2nd ed. New York: Oxford Univ. Press, 1966. A short, readable introduction to the first half of the English Reformation.

UNITY AND DIVERSITY: THE BEGINNINGS OF PROTESTANT THEOLOGY

8

In the first chapter I offered a preliminary working definition of the term *evangelical*. Since then I have used the term only rarely and usually in a fairly general way. But we have now reached a point in the narrative where the term will need to be defined more carefully.

From a historical perspective, the word *evangelical* refers to three distinct groups of people. First of all, Luther, the first of the Protestant Reformers, was known as an evangelical because of his emphasis on the *euangelion,* the good news about Jesus Christ. Lutheran churches in Germany still use the word in reference to themselves. In a broad sense all those who remain faithful to the theology taught by Luther are evangelicals.

Second, evangelicalism refers to a particular expression of Protestant Christianity which developed in the eighteenth and nineteenth centuries. In addition to a thorough commitment to Reformation theology, these evangelicals had concerns which revealed their roots in both English Puritanism and German Lutheran Pietism. Specifically, they stressed the necessity of a conscious experience of the grace of God in conversion. They were deeply concerned about spiritual renewal in the churches, the transformation of society, godly living, evangelism and missions. They accorded lay people an opportunity for significant participation in all of those concerns.

When evangelicalism in this second sense crossed the Atlantic, it took on a distinctly American cast. This was enhanced by the national origins of America's first colonists, the separation of church and state, the development of denominationalism, the existence of the frontier and the impact of the various revivals. Nonetheless, because of doctrines and emphases shared with English and European evangelicalism, the mainstream of American Protestantism, particularly as it came to fruition in the first half of the nineteenth century, can rightly share that designation.

Finally, around the turn of this century the mainstream of American Protestantism split into two camps: liberalism and fundamentalism. When the latter word was coined in 1920, it was considered almost synonymous with the word evangelicalism. Fundamentalists held to the tenets laid down by the Protestant Reformers and displayed most of the traits which were characteristic of early nineteenth-century American evangelicals. The difference centered on the fact that fundamentalism connoted protest—protest against liberal accommodations to certain intellectual trends and against the so-called social gospel. By the 1930s the fundamentalist movement was fast becoming defensive and narrow-minded. A decade later some fundamentalists began to react against that rigidity by returning to the word *evangelical* in order to dissociate themselves from some of the more extreme forms of fundamentalism. Thus arose the third use of the term. In America today, an evangelical is one who stands between liberalism and extreme fundamentalism. It refers to a person who rejects both the fundamentalist tendency toward separatism and legalism and the liberal tendency toward theological inclusiveness and neglect of the gospel in favor of direct moral action within society.

It is impossible to define the term *evangelical* simply. It meant one thing in sixteenth-century Europe; it developed a more precise meaning in nineteenth-century America; and now in the twentieth century, it has taken on additional connotations. In this chapter we will look at the sixteenth-century meaning of the word and leave later refinements to the chapters which follow.

The Authority and Clarity of the Bible

You will recall that Luther's rediscovery of the central concepts of Paul's theology was what brought him into conflict with the theology of the Roman Catholic Church and with the pope, its official defender. With much careful thought and hesitation, Luther resolved to stand against the Church. He had come to believe that the Bible alone demanded his allegiance.

The theologians of the Roman Catholic Church, on the other hand, asserted that the church had preceded the Bible. After all, the apostles were members of the body of Christ long before they wrote the Scriptures. The church had guarded those writings, and in time, the canon of the Bible was formulated and transmitted by the church. The Bible is indeed one of the church's most cherished possessions, but ultimate authority resides in the church which authenticates the Bible to individual Christians.

Luther and Calvin asserted in contradiction that the Bible is "self-authenticating." When believers read the Bible, the Spirit speaks through the text and assures them that the message comes from God. The church formed the canon, but that was merely a recognition that the Bible is the Word of the Spirit. John the Baptist pointed to Christ; his witness, however, did not make him superior to Christ. In a similar way, the church points to the Bible. The church bears witness to the fact that the Bible speaks with the authority of God himself. But the church cannot bestow that authority. The authority of the Bible does not depend in any way upon the decision of the church; the church must rather stand beneath that authority.

Furthermore, the Reformers asserted that the Scriptures are "self-interpreting" as well as self-authenticating. You recall that in order to limit the possibility of heretical interpretations of the Bible, the early Church claimed that the bishops (who are the carriers of the apostolic tradition) stand as guardians of the true interpretation of the Bible. The "teaching office" of the Church was considered necessary to protect the truth of the Christian message from perversion through misinterpretation.

This position was based on an important and controversial assumption: the Bible is inherently obscure and needs clarification by the Church. While the Reformers recognized that certain passages in the Bible are difficult to understand, they nonetheless insisted that the basic message of the Bible is crystal clear. In opposition to the stance of the Roman Catholic Church, the Reformers asserted that believers who could read could also understand the promise of salvation through faith in Jesus Christ. And that message formed the second basic element in Protestant theology.

The Rediscovery of the Gospel

Luther originally entered a monastery in order to search for his own salvation. But the conceptual framework of medieval theology would not allow him to find the peace with God that he craved. He understood salvation as the right to enter heaven and believed that God would determine who will be allowed to enter. The medieval Church taught that God is both a loving Father and a demanding Judge. The second image overshadowed the first. As Judge of the universe, God was bound to uphold justice. So Luther asked, "How can I win his favor?"

Through reading Psalms and Romans Luther began to understand that salvation is not an objective reward which God may or may not bestow. It is rather a personal reconciliation with God himself. As an expression of his love, God offers salvation (reconciliation) freely. The offer is *not* contingent in any way upon a person's ability to meet God's demands. Indeed, since people are totally incapable of fully meeting God's standards, his offer of salvation must of necessity be a gift. There is no other alternative. Consequently the essential question is not, "How can I win his favor?" but rather "How do I receive this gift of a renewed relationship?" Luther's answer stands as the central tenet of evangelical Christianity: one is justified by grace through faith in Jesus Christ.

Luther's education had taught him to understand the word *justice* as referring primarily to an aspect of God's character. It spoke of God's determination to reward righteousness and punish sin. This was a frightening concept. But Paul taught that God's justice also includes his *decision to acquit* (to justify) those of faith. In his death on the cross, Christ accepted God's just punishment for the sins of the human race. God is not merely just; he is also forgiving. The Reformers amended their understanding of justice to include this aspect.

They also redefined the concepts of *grace* and *faith.* The scholastic theologians had thought of grace as an objective reality, as that by which God modifies a person's soul. But as Luther studied Paul's letters, he saw that grace is God's coming to us in order to offer salvation. That offer is accepted by faith.

The scholastics had defined faith as "assenting to the doctrines of the church." But Luther came to see faith as primarily "trusting in God." This includes both rational and relational aspects. A person cannot trust God, a friend or anything else without first having some knowledge about the object of trust. But mere knowledge of God or mere assent to a doctrinal formulation is not sufficient. People must in addition enter into a trust relationship with God himself. Faith is the key to understanding the whole of our relationship with God.

The Catholic Church had asserted that salvation began in the sacrament of baptism. It was completed by making use of the grace available through the sacraments. In this way satisfaction was rendered to God for particular sins. In Luther's day the emphasis of the Church was on this necessity for people to complete their own salvation. But the Reformer's theology undercut the whole system. Luther saw that for Christians, salvation is an accomplished fact, assured by God's forgiveness. God always stands ready to forgive, so no one needs to live with guilt. The Reformers understood salvation as the gift of a personal relationship with God. God has declared the Christian to be innocent; salvation has been bestowed. The task of the Christian, therefore, is to implement the salvation which has been given.

Luther taught that a Christian is simultaneously a sinner and one who has been justified. God is gracious. He understands that we remain sinners even after receiving salvation. When Christians humbly ask forgiveness for sinful acts, God grants the request. Christians do not, therefore, need to be oppressed by their guilt. God's grace was bestowed in order to provide the joy of continued acceptance and forgiveness.

Luther summed up the core of his theology in two paradoxical statements: "A Christian is a perfectly free lord of all, subject to none. A Christian is a perfectly dutiful servant of all, subject to all." Luther meant that God stands ready to bestow salvation freely on all who ask in faith for his forgiveness. Christians are thus free from false confidence in their own good works and from bondage to the sacramental system as a means of attaining complete salvation. They discover that true freedom is paradoxically the loving service of all those around them.

The Ministry of Believers
The Reformers also altered the concept of priesthood. They recognized that one of the responsibilities which Christians have is that of acting as priests to neighbors. This concept of the "priesthood of all believers" is the third basic element of Protestant theology.

Now the concept of the priesthood of all believers must be defined both negatively (as freedom from) and positively (as freedom for).

The negative sense of this concept is thoroughly understood

in Protestant churches today. But it was not an accepted notion prior to Luther and Calvin. The Reformers drew the notion from the book of Hebrews (7—9) which teaches that when Jesus Christ ascended into heaven, he became our High Priest and advocate who takes our needs directly to the Father. Moreover, Christians, as adopted children, have a standing invitation to enter into the Father's presence. They do not need to go through a priest or the saints in order to speak with God. Christians have direct and immediate access to God himself through Jesus Christ. No other intermediary is necessary.

In its positive sense, the priesthood of all believers means that all Christians are called by God to act as priests to other members of the body of Christ. Here our example is Christ himself, our heavenly High Priest. Christ prayed for the disciples; we are to pray for each other. He gave himself in service to the disciples; we are to serve each other. He taught the disciples God's Word and assured them of the Father's forgiveness; we are to proclaim that promise of forgiveness to each other. Even more, we are to forgive each other. The Reformers proclaimed that all Christians are called to serve each other daily in the same way that Christ served his disciples.

If only the negative half of this concept of priesthood is remembered, the result may be religious individualism. But when the positive sense is added, when Christians see themselves as called to be priests to those around them, then the concept becomes an impetus to true religious community.

By declaring the Bible to be the final authority, by affirming that a person is saved by grace through faith in Christ and by calling all Christians to be priests for each other, the Reformers set out the basic elements of evangelical Protestant theology.

Issues Bringing Discord

On several occasions, however, individual Reformers came to different conclusions about the intent or emphasis of the Bible regarding less central issues. When that happened, unfortuately, division sometimes resulted. The Protestant Reformers were no more tolerant than others of their time.

Most of the conflicts among the Reformers originated in the area of ecclesiology, the doctrine of the church. They sometimes disagreed about the nature, task and goal of the church. These controversial issues are fascinating in their own right, but they become even more interesting when you look at them as a partial explanation for the diversity in the contemporary evangelical scene. In fact, no matter which church you choose to attend, you will probably be taught one side or the other of every one of these issues!

The significance of baptism. As we saw earlier, the theological significance of baptism brought Zwingli and the Anabaptists into public conflict. The Anabaptists noted that only adults were baptized in the New Testament and that the rite always signified a desire to repent. The rite did not, they insisted, bestow salvation. It was rather a public confession of faith. Since infants are not capable of trusting Christ and since baptism accomplishes nothing in the absence of faith, there is no reason to baptize infants. The Anabaptists asserted that the church was misguided when it began the practice of baptizing the children of confessing Christians.

Zwingli, on the other hand, responded that baptism is comparable to the Old Testament rite of circumcision. That rite was administered to infants in order to initiate them into the community of faith. From a theological point of view, both circumcision and baptism signify the promise made to the child that if he will trust God and accept God's offer of a covenant relationship, then God will grant him salvation. It is true that the child will only gradually grasp the nature and meaning of that promise. And the promise can be rejected by the child. But the promise is real nonetheless.

Luther agreed with Zwingli that baptism should be administered to children, but his reasons were quite different. He argued that since faith is a gift, God is capable of bestowing it on anyone, including infants. Both Luther and Zwingli agreed (in contrast to the Anabaptists) that baptism is more than a mere witness of faith in Jesus Christ.

Today this disagreement over the theological implications of baptism continues to divide evangelical Christians. The "free-church" or Baptist traditions continue to practice adult baptism alone while the Reformed and Lutheran traditions usually practice infant baptism. As a result, when Christians from a denomination which practices infant baptism decide to join one which practices believer's baptism, they will normally be asked to undergo rebaptism as a public profession of faith.

Understanding the Lord's Supper. Between 1524 and 1528 Luther and Zwingli engaged in a rather extended controversy regarding the theological significance of the Lord's Supper. Luther noted that Jesus had said at the Last Supper, "This *is* my body" (Lk. 22:19), not "This *signifies* my body." Consequently, when we commune with Christ in the Eucharist service, we commune with him as the God/man. He is truly present with us *in both his deity and his humanity.* Luther did not explain this phenomenon on the basis of the Catholic doctrine of transubstantiation, and he acknowledged that the experience of his senses did not square with his theology. Nonetheless, he refused the temptations to deny what he took to be the biblical teaching on the subject.

Zwingli could not accept Luther's formulation. He said that flesh which is not visible is not human flesh at all. When the Son of God took our flesh upon himself, he did so eternally. Jesus rose from the dead physically, ascended physically and sat down at the right hand of the Father. Therefore, Christians take the bread and the wine "in remembrance" of his death for us. The elements *signify* the true body of Christ. Communion, according to Zwingli, does not unite believers with Christ physically; it unites them with Christ spiritually. In addition, the rite unites members of the church with each other.

To anyone but a theologian, this whole issue may appear terribly academic. Nonetheless, because Luther and Zwingli were unable to agree, the Reformation movement was split into

Lutheran and Reformed camps. That division manifests itself today in subtle differences in the Eucharistic services within these two traditions.

Church discipline. Luther was aware from the beginning that moral standards within the church were unacceptably low, but this problem never occupied the center of his attention. He assumed that if the gospel of Jesus Christ were plainly taught from the pulpit, the whole life of the church would eventually be reformed. When Luther took a leadership role in the growing association of Lutheran churches, he emphasized the importance of the training of ministers but did not stress the need to raise moral standards.

Calvin, in contrast, believed that church leaders should take firm control of both theological education and Christian morality. He agreed with Zwingli that church leaders are responsible to teach the Bible and proclaim the biblical call to holy living. The state, in turn, was responsible to ensure that the Bible was adequately taught and followed. After Calvin took control of the Reform movement in Geneva, citizens who could not accept his teachings were forced to emigrate. In fact, at Calvin's insistence the city burned a man at the stake for his antitrinitarian theological stance. Calvin called upon the government to enforce moral principles in order to bring about a peaceful, well-ordered, Christian society.

The Anabaptists took a third approach. They asserted that the state should have no say in the internal affairs of the church, and in particular they repudiated totally the use of coercion in religious affairs. The state should enforce minimum moral standards, but it should not demand the level of holiness expected within the church. The Anabaptists agreed with Calvin that church members should live exemplary Christian lives, but they accomplished that goal by banning people from church who did not live up to high standards.

If you were to raise the question today of discipline within the church, you would probably receive a wide variety of answers. It raises the old problem of whether it is proper to judge others and whether justice or mercy should follow judgment.

The Scriptures leave room for several opinions on this complex matter.

In sum, the evangelicals of the Reformation were united by their common proclamation of the gospel of Jesus Christ. They preached the authority of the Bible, justification by grace through faith and the priesthood of all believers. On secondary issues, there was a good deal of diversity. Many of the concerns which were emphasized in the sixteenth century are also relevant today. But the term *evangelical* took on a more specialized meaning in the United States, as we shall see in the next chapter.

Further Reading

Dillenberger, John and Welch, Claude. *Protestant Christianity Interpreted through Its Development.* New York: Scribner, 1954. A short, readable history of Protestant thought which has become a standard in the field.

Hammond, T. C. *In Understanding Be Men,* 6th ed. Downers Grove, Ill.: InterVarsity Press, 1968. A readable survey of basic evangelical Protestant theology.

Marty, Martin E. *Protestantism.* Garden City, N.J.: Doubleday, Image Books, 1974. An excellent interpretive essay.

Ramm, Bernard. *The Evangelical Heritage.* Waco, Tex.: Word Books, 1973. A stimulating discussion of the theological conflicts which led to the emergence of contemporary evangelicalism.

REVIVAL AND REVOLUTION: THE FAITH IN THE UNITED STATES

9

What is an evangelical? First and foremost, evangelicals are people who believe in and live by the gospel of Jesus Christ as defined and articulated by the Protestant Reformers. It is impossible, in my opinion, to overemphasize the importance of Luther's "rediscovery" of the gospel of grace. The amount of space devoted to the Reformation indicates the importance I attach to it.

While evangelicalism is rooted firmly and securely in the Reformation, it has taken on its own distinctive shape within the American context. Much of what we understand as evangelicalism in this country originated during the first half of the nineteenth century. I would now like to examine these roots of contemporary evangelicalism.

America's Religious Diversity
To many at the time, the Elizabethan Settlement of 1559 was at

best an unfortunate and probably an unstable compromise. The Catholics who remained in England wanted to re-establish formal ties with Rome. The Puritans, the party at the other end of the continuum, felt that the Reformation in England had miscarried; they considered it a task only half done. If it had been done their way, no residue of the old Catholic ways would have been left in England. Nevertheless, the Puritans remained part of the newly created Church of England. The Anglicans, the party of the middle, saw Elizabeth's solution as a gracious compromise between two equally unsatisfactory extremes.

Toward the end of Elizabeth's reign, an even more radical group emerged from within Puritanism. These so-called separatists felt compelled to sever their ties with the state church completely, in spite of the fact that such actions were illegal. Only after separation from the Church of England, they claimed, would it be possible to institute a truly biblical religion.

In order to avoid legal problems in England, many of the separatists were forced to emigrate to Holland and then to the United States. They landed at Plymouth, Massachusetts, in 1620 where they established a church more to their liking. More moderate Puritans also sailed to the New World, but more for economic than religious reasons. They too established a church with close affinities to the Reformed churches in Europe. A decade later these two groups merged and gave birth to Congregationalism, America's first home-grown faith.

In the mid-seventeenth century, the Puritans who remained in England gained control of the government under the leadership of Oliver Cromwell. The persecuted became the persecutors. The Puritans flourished, and the Anglicans found it expedient to emigrate to the American colonies.

We usually think of America as the land of religious freedom, but history does not totally support this. The colonists who arrived in the first wave at the beginning of the seventeenth century were no more tolerant of religious diversity than their countrymen had been. But in time, some freer spirits among them began to clamor for true religious liberty. As a result the

Baptist Church emerged in Rhode Island toward the middle of the seventeenth century. Later, when northern Ireland experienced a severe economic depression, the Scotch-Irish joined the migration to the United States, bringing with them their Scottish Presbyterianism. By the year 1725, the population of the American colonies exhibited greater religious diversity than any other country in the world.

Revivalism
Revivalism was one of the key factors in the emergence of evangelicalism in America. The New England preacher and theologian Jonathan Edwards is most commonly associated with the first major revival in the United States. Edwards graduated from Yale in 1720 and took a pastorate in Northampton, Massachusetts, at a time when religious interest was at a low ebb. Because of many hours spent studying, reading and thinking, Edwards's two weekly sermons were an impressive but staid exposition of Calvin's theology. In 1734 sparks of new life began to appear. As he was delivering a series of sermons on the doctrine of justification by faith, individuals in his congregation began to sense the personal significance of this message deeply. Within a short time, the gospel became the chief topic of discussion in Northampton. God's Spirit swept through the town and brought life where there had previously been religious apathy.

The spark of revival was fanned into life again several years later by the revivalist George Whitefield. While a student at Oxford University in England, Whitefield underwent a conversion experience through his association with a student group called the "Holy Club" (its detractors called the members of the group "methodists"). After his ordination in the Church of England in 1736, Whitefield began to preach at various churches in Oxford and London. He soon gained widespread recognition as a powerful evangelistic preacher. The next year he traveled to Georgia, where this gift was again widely recognized. By 1740 he was traveling throughout New England, preaching the gospel to great crowds wherever he went. As a result of

Whitefield's preaching, the spiritual fervor awakened by Edwards was rekindled. In retrospect, the revival movement of the 1730s and 40s was named the Great Awakening.

Many sought to belittle the Great Awakening, however. Some Christian leaders considered revival meetings to be undignified shows designed to arouse emotion among the common people, and they tried to protect their churches from what they saw as an unhealthy excess. The conflict was intense. The Presbyterian Church split into two factions over the issue, and the Congregationalists divided into antagonistic parties. The issue was not one of theology. The issue centered on the importance of personal conversion—a personal response of faith in Jesus Christ. Those who disliked the revivals held that one could grow up in the church and come gradually to a Christian commitment without going through a conversion experience. Those who felt that conversion should be a part of every Christian's experience supported the revivals. Since both groups held to the theology of the Protestant Reformers, both were evangelical. But the term was applied more often to the group which emphasized the conversion experience. Today, some two hundred years later, that stress on personal experience is still highly characteristic of evangelicalism.

John Wesley also made an important contribution to American evangelicalism in the eighteenth century. Like Whitefield, he attended Oxford and participated in the Holy Club, but he did not experience conversion until much later. He was ordained in the Church of England and in 1735 came to the United States. But, unlike Whitefield, Wesley returned to England without having achieved much because he himself had not yet experienced spiritual rebirth. After returning to London in 1738, Wesley attended a small chapel meeting at which Luther's *Preface to the Book of Romans* was read. According to his own later report, his heart was warmed during the reading, and his conversion that night transformed his whole life. He traveled throughout England preaching the Word of God with great power among the people until his death in 1791. He never returned to the United States, but his theology became a major element in American evangelical thought.

Edwards and Whitefield were staunch advocates of Calvin's doctrine of predestination. According to that doctrine God chooses some and enables them to come to Christ and leaves others to damnation according to his own sovereign will. Wesley, in contrast, was Arminian in his theology; that is, he accepted the views of Jacob Arminius who taught that each person must freely choose to respond to God's grace in order to experience salvation. Wesley affirmed that no person would—or could— turn to God without God's grace. But he placed the emphasis on choice. He taught that the way in which people respond to the gospel is the decisive factor in their salvation.

Furthermore, Wesley articulated a theology built around the phrase "Christian perfection." Every Christian, he claimed, needs to undergo a second experience of grace after salvation in which God completes his work and brings true holiness to life. Absolute perfection may not be attainable in this life, but Christians can and must become free from voluntary transgression of known law. In time the Methodist societies which Wesley formed to encourage true holiness of life among his converts spread to the American colonies.

Impact of the American Revolution
The generation after the Great Awakening witnessed the gradual deterioration of political ties between the colonies and England which culminated in revolution and independence. Since most of the religious groups in the United States had formal relationships with parent churches in Europe, each group had to form an independent national body after the war. Because of the number of different religious affiliations, the new, independent government could not create a national church like those in Europe. That situation led to the emergence in America of the denomination, a voluntary association of churches unsupported by the government. This characteristic (voluntarism) and the separation of church and state have contributed to the

proliferation of denominations in America.

As the United States entered the nineteenth century, Protestant leaders began to recognize that the religious diversity in the United States was not only permanent but also a potential source of strength. The same gospel was preached by all of the evangelical denominations. The differences were tolerable. The denominations disagreed about matters such as the proper form for church government, the doctrine of predestination or the importance of infant baptism, but they agreed on the importance of bringing the gospel of Christ to all individuals. That tacit agreement constituted the core of the "evangelical consensus." By the turn of the nineteenth century, evangelical Protestantism had become the religious mainstream of the United States. Never embodied in a permanent ecclesiastical unit, it was rather a style or a distinctive way of being Protestant. That distinctiveness stands out most clearly when evangelicalism is contrasted with its theological alternatives, examined as a religious force on the expanding frontier and seen in its influence on society.

Evangelicalism and Its Theological Alternatives
During the eighteenth century, some of the clergy within the New England Congregational Church began to question the classic formulations of the doctrine of Christ. They acknowledged the Bible as the record of God's successive revelations to mankind but insisted that it had been misread and misused by the church. In particular, these ministers rejected the doctrine of Christ's dual nature. He was not, in their opinion, the God/man. Furthermore, they denied the doctrine of the atonement; that is, the belief that Christ was a sacrifice for the sins of the whole world. Their position became known in time as Unitarianism. Their rejection of the deity of Jesus Christ and the concept of atonement placed them in opposition to evangelicals who continued to hold both doctrines.

Second, evangelicals continued to see themselves in opposition to the Roman Catholic Church over the same issues which had divided the Church during the Reformation. Evangelicals stood for the right of individuals to read and interpret the Word of God while Catholics insisted on the importance of the "teaching office" of the Church. The evangelicals insisted also that individuals must respond to the gospel in faith in order to experience God's saving work.

Third, they continued to oppose various quasi-Christian sects which sprang up in the United States during this century. Some groups formed themselves around new claims to revelation. A man named Joseph Smith, for example, claimed to have received a series of revelations during the 1820s which are recorded in the *Book of Mormon*. These new teachings formed the basis for the Church of Latter-day Saints. Other groups experimented with communal living based on broadly religious, but not Christian, ideas. The Oneida Community, formed by John Humphrey Noyes near Syracuse, New York, was a good case in point. Finally, some individuals dabbled in spiritualism.

Lastly, evangelicals continued to oppose—albeit in a more brotherly sort of way—Protestants who taught proper theology but neglected evangelistic preaching. Evangelicals valued biblical preaching which called for a personal response.

Expansion on the Frontier

Just before 1800 settlers began surging westward. Since few of them had been formally affiliated with an organized church, a need developed for a religious influence on the frontier. God's Spirit began to move, and just as the new century was beginning, the country was swept by the Second Great Awakening.

James McGready, a Presbyterian minister who went west in 1796, settled in Logan County, Kentucky, where he served three churches. Over the next four years a spark of revival appeared and gradually grew as a result of his preaching. In 1800 the preaching of a nearby Methodist minister named John McGee began to attract people from farther away. In fact, some people came and stayed for several days in order to hear more. In this small way the "camp meeting" was born.

Barton W. Stone, a Presbyterian minister in Bourbon County,

Kentucky, visited Logan County to see what God was doing there. He returned home to preach revival. Sometime later fifteen or twenty thousand people came for his meeting at Cane Ridge in Bourbon County. Some of what occurred there would strike the twentieth-century reader as bizarre, but God's Spirit was at work. Many participants returned home with a lasting conviction of the importance of spiritual growth and personal holiness.

In the years that followed, camp meetings were held throughout the frontier in order to bring the gospel to settlers.

The frontier churches were forced to develop a whole new approach to ministry because the population was highly dispersed. The Methodist Church commissioned circuit riders to bring teaching, preaching and worship to widely separated congregations. The Baptists licensed lay people to preach in their home churches. When these people moved west, they took their Bibles and licenses to preach and formed new congregations wherever they settled. Through such unsophisticated but practical methods the West was gradually brought under the influence of the gospel.

In such a context education was not highly regarded. As the frontier moved west, the Baptist farmer/preacher moved along with it while those with more education tended to remain behind. In time, some churches generalized from that pattern and concluded that education was unnecessary. God seemed to be able to work quite well without it. That attitude, deduced from the necessities of the frontier era, continues to appear from time to time among evangelicals today.

Worship services were simple and unadorned. For obvious reasons it was not possible on the frontier to have a choir, a fine building or beautiful vestments for the minister. If the gospel was preached and people were won to Christ, the church was a success. No more could be asked in such a transient situation. To this day, many evangelical congregations maintain that simplicity and informality.

Revival began in the East almost simultaneously with the Cane

Ridge meetings. The movement of God's Spirit began at Yale College in 1802 with the preaching of the college president, Timothy Dwight. As a result a whole generation of future leaders felt the pull of the Spirit. The movement of God's Spirit utterly shattered the spiritual lethargy that had gripped the country and the newly formed denominations in the decade or two following the war for independence.

Throughout the colonial period Presbyterians and Baptists taught Calvin's theology. But at the onset of the nineteenth century, John Wesley's holiness theology began to penetrate the frontier through the efforts of the Methodist circuit riders. It is ironic that one of the most important early advocates of holiness theology prior to the Civil War was a Presbyterian by background—Charles Grandison Finney. Finney began to practice law in central New York in 1818 and simultaneously started to study the Bible for himself. Three years later his studies produced a soul-shaking conversion, and he committed himself immediately to pleading the case for Jesus Christ.

Finney was an immediate success as an evangelist, and after only a few years the Presbyterian Church ordained him to the ministry. Unlike previous Presbyterian revivalists, Finney emphasized the importance of the human element and taught the doctrine of Christian perfection. In 1835 he accepted an invitation to become professor of theology at the newly formed Oberlin College where he was given the freedom to teach his own approach to theology and evangelism. In time his ideas, known subsequently as "Oberlin theology," became an important element in the evangelical theological perspective.

In sum, early nineteenth-century evangelicalism was extremely diverse. Baptists and Presbyterians taught traditional Reformed theology while Methodists and the followers of Finney taught holiness doctrine. Denominations split and re-formed as they worked to win the frontier for Christ. The church on the frontier found it essential to dispense with ritual and an educated clergy. Yet in spite of its diversity, its tendency to fragment and the low educational level of its frontier clergy, evangelicalism proved capable of expanding and advancing. What evangelicals had in common was their concern for calling people to commitment to Jesus Christ and to personal moral reformation. The message they preached was the source of their strength.

Evangelicals in Society

Evangelical Christians of the early 1800s were activists by inclination. They channeled their energies into a whole network of interdenominational, voluntary associations formed to implement their vision of a truly Christian society. These included missions, educational activities and social reform.

Missions. The year 1806 marked the real beginning of American evangelical involvement in foreign missions. While out walking one day, Samuel J. Mills and several other students from Williams College took shelter from a rainstorm under a haystack and used the time to pray about foreign missions. Following that famous "haystack prayer meeting," the group became instrumental in bringing into existence the American Board of Commissioners for Foreign Missions. Subsequently, American evangelicals provided the major impetus for the Protestant missionary movement.

Education. At the beginning of the nineteenth century, only rare frontier families had Bibles. The American Bible Society (modeled after a British counterpart) was formed in 1816 to more adequately meet the need, and within a few years over a hundred thousand Bibles were distributed. The American Tract Society was also formed at that time to provide Christian literature for the growing population.

Sunday schools had first appeared in England toward the end of the eighteenth century but did not cross the Atlantic until early in the nineteenth century. Evangelicals organized the American Sunday School Union to produce and distribute materials for use in local churches. As the frontier moved west, numerous colleges and seminaries were formed in its wake to upgrade the educational level of the ministry in the growing evangelical constituency.

Social reform. Evangelicals constantly tried to apply the gospel to moral issues for social change. For example, evangelicals formed numerous societies to control or suppress activities which seemed to them to be harmful to society. The American Society for the Promotion of Temperance was one of many created at that time.

Moreover, some of the nineteenth-century evangelicals took a strong, public stand against the social and institutional evils which permeated society at large. Finney, for example, while more frequently remembered for his work in evangelism, was a radical social critic. In his *Lectures on Revivals of Religion* he listed a variety of "hindrances to revival," one of which was "taking the wrong ground on questions of human rights." What he had in mind was slavery. He insisted that Christians were obligated to take a public stand against that evil. Moreover, he argued that Christians involved in the "social sin of slaveholding" should be excluded from the Lord's Supper and placed under the discipline of the church. Oberlin College was begun by students as a "free seminary" in protest against those who would limit the right to speak out on slavery. Finney's decision to teach at Oberlin was tantamount to taking a public stand with those radical students. The early peace movement and the movement for women's rights similarly received the attention of evangelicals.

The evangelicals of the early 1800s had roots in the Reformed tradition, but they included a growing Arminian/holiness wing. They encompassed a variety of Protestant denominations, but they all held the common conviction that Christians must actively take the gospel to those who have not yet heard. That conviction led to evangelism, revivals and camp meetings on the frontier, as well as a growing interest in foreign missions. Furthermore, they agreed that a commitment to Jesus Christ should be translated into moral reform and corporate social action.

Racial Diversification in the Churches
The spread of Christianity on the frontier was accompanied by the establishment of churches among free blacks and slaves.

One of the greatest paradoxes in the spread of Christianity was its close association with the institution of slavery in America. Although some Christians fought relentlessly for the abolition of this institution, others ran to Scripture to defend what they believed to be God's plan for the African "heathens." Tragically, the African slaves' first introduction to Christianity came on the decks of slave ships, at plantation missions and in the so-called nigger pews at the churches of their white masters.

The Africans who survived the horrors of the Atlantic crossing brought with them a distinct cultural and religious heritage. Yet in time this heritage took on new forms and expressions as the slaves were not allowed to maintain their native languages and tribal relationships. Christianity slowly supplanted the traditional religions of the slaves and gave them an important entrée into the American colonial scene.

As blacks began to give Christianity their own distinct interpretations, they often noted the difference between true Christianity and the religion of the slaveholders. Many of the sermons of white plantation preachers exhorted slaves to be submissive and obedient to their masters. But the religion of the slaves focused on the God who promised freedom for all his children—in this world and the next. The spirituals gave expression to the soul of this black Christianity. The slaves sang of One who comforted the motherless child and assured the relatives of broken families that they would see their mothers and fathers again one day. In short, black Christianity provided an oasis in the midst of the slave wilderness; it was a reservoir of strength for those who were treated as chattel.

Through the efforts of the Baptist and Methodist missionaries, the population of the black Christian community increased. It was not too long before serious tensions developed between white parishioners and their slaves. A call for the development of separate black churches under the leadership of recognized black preachers was soon heard in several denominations. As a result, about the time of the Revolutionary War one of the first black Baptist Churches was organized in the Savannah,

Georgia area under the leadership of George Liele and Andrew Bryan. However, one of the critical points in the evolution of independent black churches occurred in the experiences of two ministers—Richard Allen and Absalom Jones.

Allen, born a slave in Philadelphia in 1760, was converted by a Methodist preacher in 1777. Soon afterward he was allowed to purchase his freedom, and he became a preacher. In 1786, Allen, Jones and other blacks walked out of a service at St. George's Methodist Church in Philadelphia after a heated confrontation with the ushers. The black leaders had knelt to pray in the white section of the balcony and were physically removed from there by irate white ushers.

As a result of this secession, Allen formed Bethel Church and in 1794 renovated an old building to serve its needs. Other black Methodist Churches were formed, and in 1816 they became an official denomination—the African Methodist Episcopal Church. Richard Allen became their first bishop. Reverend Absalom Jones left the Methodists to assume leadership of the African Protestant Episcopal Church of St. Thomas. Racial separation, then, became the paradigm of American church relations and development.

For the rest of the nineteenth century, the burgeoning black church and its leaders took up the critical issues of the day, fighting for the abolition of slavery, the universal equality of mankind, and the moral and spiritual improvement of black people. After the Civil War, these black churches joined the efforts of northern whites to secure education and jobs for the newly freed blacks. Black churches were also among the first churches in America to send missionaries overseas.

At the close of the nineteenth century, the majority of the black population was still located in the South, struggling to survive despite the injustices of segregation and the Jim Crow laws. But the devastating effects of the boll weevil in the South, the need for laborers in northern factories and the promise of a better life brought thousands of blacks to northern cities early in the twentieth century. Black preachers and churches followed their people to places like Harlem, Philadelphia and Chicago.

The northern black churches did not always satisfy the spiritual appetites of the southern migrants. As a result, several black sects blossomed on ghetto corners. While some of the sects (for example, that of Sweet Daddy Grace) prepared their members to accept discrimination; others, like the Black Muslims, encouraged their followers to reject segregated Christianity and to establish an economic base for blacks. Ministers like Adam Clayton Powell, Sr., in the best of the black church tradition, served the spiritual, social, political and economic needs of blacks.

In the early years of the twentieth century, some conservative Christians reacted against liberal theology, which was identified with a stress on social action to the exclusion of individual salvation, by saying that the church should not be involved in social and political activities (see p. 147). But conservative black churches, for the most part, did not espouse this viewpoint. Black Christians felt the need to minister and to be ministered to as whole persons—that is, as people with physical and emotional needs as well as spiritual ones. This union of social action and evangelism has continued to be an earmark of black evangelicalism in the United States.

Challenge and Disintegration

Prior to the Civil War, evangelical Protestantism had constituted the religious mainstream of the United States. But between the end of the war and the turn of the century, the evangelical consensus began to disintegrate.

The frontier continued to move west and to challenge the church's capacity to reach the unevangelized. Simultaneously the urban population began to explode, and a whole new complex of problems was created. The evangelical denominations which had geared up to evangelize the frontier were not able to move with vigor into the cities. And the flow of immigrants into the cities continued and even increased.

Perhaps the greatest challenge presented to evangelicalism during this period was an intellectual one. Because they had devoted their efforts to winning the frontier for Christ, evangelicals were unprepared to meet the intellectual challenges which arose. In 1859, Darwin published *The Origin of the Species*. Although this book did not directly challenge the church's understanding of God and creation, the speculations which arose from it tended to discount the role of a Creator in the origins of life. Furthermore, throughout the century a steady stream of writings representing the German critical approach to the Bible (see pp. 38-39) circulated in the United States. The method of biblical interpretation which this so-called higher criticism represented was not inherently antithetical to Christianity. But the presuppositions of those who used the method often were. As a result it tended to undermine evangelical beliefs about the Bible's origins.

By the end of the nineteenth century, the evangelical consensus had begun to divide over how to respond to these issues. On the one hand, a group of "evangelical liberals" tried to accommodate themselves to the intellectual challenges of the period while maintaining traditional beliefs such as the deity of Christ and the authority of the Bible. But this effort took some of them over the boundary of orthodoxy into more radical alternatives. More conservative evangelicals, in an effort to resist the tide which swept some evangelical liberals into unbelief, tended to be overly cautious and even reactionary. This set the stage for the so-called fundamentalist-modernist controversy of the early twentieth century.

The Conservative Response

Three important issues within contemporary American evangelicalism find their origins in the conservative reaction to liberal challenges.

Inerrancy. Throughout the nineteenth century Princeton Theological Seminary had been a major conservative bulwark against the growing trend toward a more liberal theology. As more liberal scholars used higher criticism to attack a simplistic faith in the Bible, the Princeton theologians fought knowledgeably for the authority of Scripture and became known for their defense of the "inerrancy" of the Bible. This was not a new concept; in fact, the idea goes back at least to the Lutheran orthodoxy of the seventeenth century. The novelty was in the intensity of their commitment to that particular word. B. B. Warfield, one of the most famous defenders of the Princeton view, pointed out that the concept of inerrancy can apply only to the original documents since everyone recognizes that the present copies of the Bible may contain errors. Hence the phrase *the inerrancy of the autographs* was used to defend the authority of the Bible against its attackers. That theological position became a central tenet of fundamentalist doctrine.

Eschatology. A second characteristic of evangelicalism which appeared during that period was a growing fascination with biblical prophecy and eschatology (the doctrine of the "end times"). One of the theological threads which runs through the Old Testament is God's promise to the Jews that he would establish an earthly kingdom of peace and prosperity for them. Since about the second or third century, the church had generally taught that those promises should be interpreted figuratively, to apply to the church rather than the Jewish state. The church must be seen as a spiritual Israel. Christ would indeed return to render judgment, but he would then initiate the heavenly kingdom. There would be no literal, earthly reign of peace and prosperity (known as the millennium) such as the Jews had expected. That position was called amillennialism.

Toward the close of the nineteenth century, a growing number of people began to advocate the premillennial position. That doctrine had appeared throughout the history of the church, but it had not been widely accepted. The position stated that Christ was coming soon and would set up his kingdom here on earth and reign for a thousand years. Prophecy conferences were held with growing frequency and enthusiasm. Still others held to postmillennialism, the belief that Christ's return would *follow* a period (though not necessarily a thousand years) of spiritual prosperity (see also pp. 155-57).

Christian perfection. The third trait to be noted here is the continued growth of the holiness movement. The doctrine of Christian perfection had first appeared in the theology of John Wesley and was carried on by the evangelist Charles Finney (see pp. 132 and 137). After the Civil War, holiness theology began to attract growing numbers of people. In the summer of 1867, a camp meeting was held which was devoted to the doctrine of "entire sanctification." At the meeting, a holiness association was formed in order to propagate the doctrine. During the next twenty years, over sixty camp meetings were held under its auspices.

This growth created a controversy within the Methodist denomination. The emotionalism associated with camp meetings offended some people, while others considered entire sanctification an essential part of their Methodist heritage. Eventually, those who fought against the holiness doctrine triumphed in the denomination, and thousands of members left in order to found dozens of small holiness churches. The conflict over the doctrine of Christian perfection made evangelicalism just slightly more complex.

Further Reading

Dayton, Donald W. *Discovering an Evangelical Heritage.* New York: Harper & Row, 1976. A short study of evangelical social involvement during the nineteenth century. Contains some surprising material.

Frazier, E. Franklin. *The Negro Church in America* and Lincoln, C. Eric. *The Black Church Since Frazier,* one-volume ed. New York: Schocken Books, 1963 and 1974. An updated version of a basic text in black church history.

Gaustad, Edwin Scott. *A Religious History of America.* New York: Harper & Row, 1974. A good introduction to religion in America.

Sandeen, Ernest R. *The Roots of Fundamentalism: British and American Millenarianism, 1800-1930.* Chicago: Univ. of Chicago Press, 1970. Somewhat scholarly, but well written and accessible to lay people.

Synan, Vinson. *The Holiness-Pentecostal Movement in the United States.* Grand Rapids: Eerdmans, 1971. A solid history of the holiness-Pentecostal wing of evangelicalism.

NEITHER WATERED DOWN NOR SET IN CONCRETE: CONTEMPORARY AMERICAN EVANGELICALISM

10

Contemporary American evangelicalism is most often understood as being closely linked to the fundamentalist movement. In fact, contemporary evangelicalism did emerge out of fundamentalism. Today, however, it is seen as a distinct phenomenon which developed in reaction to the extreme fundamentalism of the 1930s.

The Origins of Fundamentalism
Between 1910 and 1915 a series of twelve small volumes entitled *The Fundamentals* were sent to clergy and theological students throughout the United States as a gift from two wealthy Christian brothers, Milton and Lyman Stewart. The three million pieces of literature which were thus distributed changed the face of American Protestantism.

The Fundamentals contained a collection of articles written by a diverse group of conservative evangelicals in an attempt to articulate the central affirmations of the gospel message. Roughly one-third of the articles were devoted to defending the verbal inspiration and authority of the Bible. An equal number dealt with the essential doctrines of the faith, such as the deity of Christ, his virgin birth, his substitutionary atonement, his bodily resurrection, and his imminent and visible return. The final third recounted personal testimony or dealt with topics such as missions, evangelism and the relationship between science and the Christian faith. Both the writers and the publishers felt *The Fundamentals* enunciated the very core of the gospel. They felt that any effort to expound the Christian faith without that core would be a compromise and a serious threat to the integrity of the message. The books were both a positive statement of the fundamentals of the faith and a defense of conservative theology against liberal criticism. Thus, conservative evangelicals came to be called fundamentalists.

In opposition liberal Protestants insisted that Christianity must take into consideration recent discoveries in science and biblical criticism. They advocated forming a positive synthesis between the old orthodoxy and the new theories. The fundamentalists argued that accommodation had the potential for destroying the Christian faith. One cannot jettison biblical teachings regarding the virgin birth or the resurrection, for example, in a misguided attempt to amalgamate the faith with nineteenth-century naturalism. The two are not compatible.

As a result of this ongoing controversy, some of the fundamentalists became much more defensive in orientation after about 1920. Many of them fastened on the theory of evolution as a particularly insidious manifestation of secularism and naturalism. The issue came to a head in the famous Scopes trial of 1925. The American Civil Liberties Union (ACLU) convinced John T. Scopes to test the new Tennessee law which forbade the teaching of evolution in public schools. The widely publicized trial pitted the nationally known fundamentalist lawyer and Populist politician William Jennings Bryan against Clarence Darrow, the ACLU lawyer and representative of modern skepticism. Scopes was convicted and fined. But while the fundamentalists won in court, they failed in their bid for public support. To most Americans, they appeared reactionary.

During the next ten years the fundamentalist movement retreated slowly and defensively from the Protestant mainstream. The battle for control of the denominations was bitter, and a few groups split as a direct result of the controversy. The majority of conservatives remained in their denominations, but limited their involvement. Some fundamentalist leaders became militant separatists. Their perception of a growing attack on the gospel impelled them to separate from liberalism totally and completely. Furthermore, some leaders insisted that fundamentalists should separate themselves not only from liberals but also from conservatives who compromised the gospel by associating with liberals.

Fundamentalists and Evangelicals
By the mid-thirties the more moderate fundamentalists began to sense a growing cleavage between their position and that of the militants. The connotations of the word *fundamentalist* had changed significantly between 1920 and 1935. Along with their legitimate concern to defend the faith, fundamentalists had acquired some attitudes which were less acceptable. For instance, they underrated the intellectual side of life. The so-called higher criticism and the theory of evolution were propagated in the centers of higher education. So fundamentalists often disparaged the university and sent their children to Bible institutes. Furthermore, they saw that an overemphasis on the social implications of the gospel in liberal circles tended to hinder the proclamation of the good news. Here again, fundamentalists overreacted by denying the appropriateness of speaking out for justice and equality in society. They also tended to become fiercely conservative politically.

Reacting against these extrabiblical values, some of the moderate fundamentalists returned to the more historic term, *evangelical,* around 1940. To call oneself an evangelical now implied a rejection of the separatist mentality and defensiveness which had become characteristic of fundamentalism. Yet both fundamentalists and evangelicals continued to teach and maintain the fundamentals of the faith.

How, then, was the evangelical mentality different? The philosophy espoused by Billy Graham's evangelistic organization might be taken as typical. Graham consistently proclaimed the doctrine of original sin and the need for an intelligent commitment to Jesus Christ. This placed him in opposition to more liberal expressions of the faith. Yet he was willing to work with denominational groups which have a liberal wing in order to plan and promote his evangelistic campaigns. His stance has drawn consistent criticism from the fundamentalist right.

Shortly after the Second World War, American evangelicals began to recognize the importance of enunciating and defending the gospel with intellectual vigor. A trickle of evangelical literature began to appear. Not only did evangelicals recognize the need for university education, but groups like Inter-Varsity Christian Fellowship provided opportunities for evangelism and fellowship among university students. In 1947, Fuller Theological Seminary was organized to provide quality evangelical education on the graduate level. Then in 1956 *Christianity Today* was founded to provide a vehicle for expressing the evangelical theological stance. Since the sixties and early seventies, the faculties of the evangelical seminaries have been producing a veritable tidal wave of quality evangelical literature.

In the last decade or so, evangelicals have begun to recognize that many of their nineteenth-century forebears were thoroughly involved in dealing with the problems and social issues of their day. Evangelicals have, as a result, begun to question their own lack of involvement. Today, they are increasingly aware that they are responsible to fight for justice and to demonstrate concern for people in tangible ways.

Evangelical Theology: The Controversial Issues

A creative alternative to the fundamentalist-modernist polarity could not appear if that old controversy were merely ignored. Yet the effort to work out a moderate solution entailed debate and disagreement. When that effort was carried out in a spirit of love, it produced real growth in our understanding of a truly biblical theology. But at times the discussions degenerated into acrimony and bitterness.

Some of the issues in evangelical thought today originated in the fundamentalist-modernist controversy. These include biblical inerrancy, creation and evolution, the place of prophecy, the significance of spiritual gifts, the role of women and the relationship of evangelism and social action. There is not room to discuss all of these issues here, and my purpose is not to offer solutions. But I will examine a few issues because they have had lengthy histories and they continue to spark heated discussions in evangelical circles.

The inspiration and authority of the Bible. The philosophical rationalism of the eighteenth century led in the nineteenth century to an intellectual and political climate in which one could safely criticize traditional ideas about the Bible. For the first time scholars could speak their minds with impunity. The first point to come under criticism was the belief that Moses wrote the Pentateuch. Later, the historical accuracy of the gospel accounts was challenged. The church was forced to respond, and this response led to a polarization within mainstream evangelical Protestantism at the end of the nineteenth century.

Today evangelical scholars are still searching for a creative answer to the challenge posed by the methods of higher criticism. Two new elements give some promise. First, many of the faculty members of the major evangelical theological seminaries were at least partly educated within a liberal environment. Most of these evangelical scholars have maintained close contact with their liberal mentors and know that they are, in general, scholars of intellectual honesty and integrity. As a result, the lines of communication are much more open than they sometimes were between the fundamentalists and the liberals. Second, evangelical scholars have begun to think and write about some of the serious, puzzling problems within Scripture. They have come to appreciate the methods of higher criticism without adopting its presuppositions, and they have recognized that liberal theologians often have strong, though unconvincing, arguments for their positions.

Several evangelical positions on the inspiration and authority of the Bible have emerged from this dialog with liberal theologians. The first asserts that since the Bible is inerrant, the text must mean literally what it says. Those who take this approach would insist, for instance, that Solomon wrote the book of Ecclesiastes. Liberal theologians had insisted that the author of Ecclesiastes, who calls himself the "son of David," must have lived much later than Solomon's time because of the advanced linguistic expressions he uses. Evangelicals who hold the first (literal, inerrant) position would insist that there are ways of interpreting the linguistic evidence which are consistent with the affirmation that Solomon, son of King David, was the author. Furthermore, these evangelical scholars sometimes charge that Christians who hedge on this point by appealing to the "intent" of the author (and thereby allowing for authorship by someone other than Solomon) are denying the authority of the Bible.

A second, more recent school of thought suggests that the word *inerrant* may be a stumbling block. Inerrancy is, in their opinion, an unfortunate theological stance which developed when the Scriptures were under attack. But it is not, they assert, the best possible response to the problem. One should speak rather of the authority and infallibility of the Bible. Evangelicals of this school insist that the Bible is in fact God's Word. When we read the words of the Bible, those words tell us of God's message of salvation in such a way that we hear exactly what God intended us to hear. Most of the evangelical scholars who take this approach would be comfortable with the argument that the person (not Solomon) who wrote Ecclesiastes used a literary form whereby a writer would attribute his work to a historical personage. This ambiguity in authorship would have presented no problem to the *original* readers. It should not, therefore, present a problem for us. And the intent of the writer is clear.

The evangelicals in the middle argue that the term *inerrancy* is necessary in order to protect the authority of the Word against liberal inroads. But they would also insist that the concept of the "intent of the author" is necessary in order to avoid reading more into the text than the original writer actually placed there. Those who hold this position within the evangelical spectrum would probably be divided among themselves over the issue of the authorship of Ecclesiastes that I have used as an illustration.

Creation and evolution. By 1920 or so, the critique of the theory of evolution had been joined in the fundamentalist mind with the defense of the faith. The passage of the antievolution law in Tennessee which resulted in the Scopes trial was not an isolated phenomenon. During the early twenties, conservative Christians mounted an intensive, nationwide attempt to exclude the theory of evolution from public education, and that attempt was successful in several states. The movement reached its apex when the fundamentalists won the Scopes trial. But their victory was marred by the fact that the laws which banned instruction about evolution were widely ignored afterward.

This particular controversy came to be seen as a case in point of the larger controversy about the inspiration and authority of the Bible. The fundamentalists attempted to force conservative Protestants to see all evolutionary theory as irreconcilably opposed to the belief that the first chapters of the Bible are God's Word. But evangelicals have refused to believe that they must choose between the Bible and science; so the controversy continues. Fuel has been added to the fires of disagreement as recently as 1969 when the textbook committee of the California State Board of Education passed a petition describing creation as a scientific theory which should be taught along with evolution. The resulting hubbub involved Christians (scientists and teachers) on both sides of the issue.

Evangelicals agree that since the Bible is the Word of God, the creation account cannot be taken lightly. But they remain divided about how to reconcile evolutionary theory with the first chapters of Genesis. Some evangelicals agree with the fundamentalists that the world was created by God in six days around 4000 B.C. They account for fossil remains and geologic strata by saying that a catastrophic flood, recounted in Genesis 6—9, disrupted the original created order.

Most evangelicals, however, search for a mediating stance which maintains the authority of the Bible while working with the conclusions of the scientific community. Many of them accept those portions of evolutionary theory which are well supported, including the assertion that our world developed its present form gradually over an extremely long period of time.

Some evangelicals, for example, interpret the term *day* as referring to a geologic age. They argue that the text of Genesis itself precludes a literal interpretation by referring to "days" prior to the creation of the sun and moon on the fourth "day." Thus, they hold that God used natural processes to create the world in six distinct steps, but each step took many thousands of years. Another theory is that God created the world over many thousands of years, but *revealed* it to the author of Genesis in six, twenty-four-hour days.

Finally, some evangelicals deny the *possibility* of a conflict between the Genesis account and recent scientific theories. They see the creation account as a theological discussion of the nature of God and man and of their relationship. According to this interpretation, the author of Genesis intentionally recast a creation story which was circulating in the ancient Near East in order to contrast Yahweh with the gods of the pagan nations around Israel. The account was not, therefore, intended by the author to speak historically about creation, but rather about the creative God of Israel.

The advocates of each of these approaches agree that what God has said to us in his Word is true. They disagree about how these particularly difficult chapters should be interpreted.

The place of spiritual gifts. During a revival held at the Azusa Street Church in Los Angeles in 1906, numerous people claimed to have been "baptized by the Holy Spirit." They said, furthermore, that their newly acquired ability to speak in "tongues" should be accepted as evidence for their statements. (To outsiders, the gift of tongues sounds like a very fluent, even melodious murmuring. Those who exhibit this gift of the Spirit frequently claim that the sounds which are uttered are in fact an actual language, even when there is no one present who can identify it. The gift is considered most useful when utilized in conjunction with interpretation or in private prayers to God.) This phenomenon attracted wide public attention and the theological issues it raised quickly became the cause of another controversy within contemporary evangelicalism.

The new movement found its historical antecedence in the New Testament book of Acts. Acts 2 records a complex of extraordinary events which transpired in Jerusalem on the day of Pentecost shortly after Jesus Christ ascended into heaven. The Holy Spirit came upon the Christians present, and those who received the gift of the Holy Spirit manifested several notable signs. One of those signs was the gift of tongues. This gift enabled the apostles to preach the message of Christ in a variety of languages to Jews from various countries who were visiting Jerusalem for the feast day.

The Christians at the Azusa Street revival asserted that God did not intend spiritual gifts to be limited to those living at the time of the apostles. God intended the baptism of the Holy Spirit and the gift of tongues to be for Christians of all times. Every Christian should, therefore, be open to receiving the Holy Spirit and speaking in tongues, the unique sign of the Spirit's presence.

The Azusa Street revival had roots in the holiness movement which was discussed in chapter nine. The leaders of the movement were consequently attuned to the idea of a second work of grace. But this phenomenon, they claimed, was something else altogether. The holiness movement had emphasized a second work of grace, which led to purification from sin. The leaders at Azusa Street, however, claimed that the baptism of the Holy Spirit is yet another work in which God provides the Christian with the power necessary for effective Christian service.

The Pentecostal movement, which grew out of the revival, took the stand that speaking in tongues is an outward sign of the inward filling of the Holy Spirit and that other manifestations of the presence of the Spirit (such as the gifts of healing or prophecy) were also possible. The individuals who had experienced this Pentecostal power began to form denominations in which their distinctive theology could be freely taught.

The early Pentecostals thought of themselves as fundamentalists. Fundamentalists, however, were not open to their teaching. Most fundamentalists were advocates of a dispensational theology which teaches that the special gifts of the Spirit, such as tongues, healing and prophecy, belong solely to the apostolic age, not to the present age. So for many years Pentecostals were not accepted in conservative Christian circles. It was not until the formation of the National Association of Evangelicals (1942) that better communication between Pentecostals and other evangelical Christians was established.

After about 1960 Pentecostal theology gained articulate advocates within both the mainline Protestant denominations and the Roman Catholic Church. This recent activity is usually called Neo-Pentecostalism or the charismatic movement (from the Greek word *charismata* which means "gifts"). The explosive growth of the movement has forced the larger evangelical community to grapple with this doctrinal innovation.

Advocates of charismatic theology claim to have noted a scriptural truth which the church had systematically and intentionally ignored. They claim, furthermore, that the corporate experience of twentieth-century Pentecostals justifies their claim that the baptism of the Holy Spirit is real and that the gifts of the Spirit are available to Christians today. Fully convinced by their own experiences, they tend to perceive those who oppose their teachings as resistant to the work of the Holy Spirit.

On the other hand, evangelical theologians who are not charismatic have tended to deny that charismatic theology is truly biblical. They have insisted that personal experience must never be allowed to determine doctrine. In consequence, the zeal of the charismatics has frequently met with an equally zealous repudiation. Many congregations in the United States have split over this issue.

In recent years, however, encouraging discussions have occurred, and a reconciliation seems to be in the making. Many charismatics have recognized that it is unbiblical to insist that all Christians speak in tongues. The larger evangelical community, meanwhile, has begun to recognize that God has used the baptism of the Holy Spirit to transform the lives of many Christians. While one may want to discuss alternative ways of articulating those experiences theologically, no one should deny the obvious work of the Spirit of God through them.

Biblical prophecy and dispensational theology. In the last chapter I noted that one sector of nineteenth-century American evangelicalism developed a strong interest in the subject of eschatology, the doctrine of the "last things" or end times. In the century since then, that interest has become an abiding fascination. As a result it would be impossible to communicate the full flavor of contemporary evangelicalism without noting the interest in biblical prophecy within that community. The fact that a recent book on the subject (*The Late Great Planet Earth* by Hal Lindsey) sold several million copies in the United States indicates that the subject is of more than passing interest.

About midway through the nineteenth century, John N. Darby, an English evangelical, developed a unique theological approach to the Bible known as "dispensationalism." Darby traveled throughout the Midwestern and Eastern sections of the United States during the third quarter of that century in order to propagate his theology. He was very successful. Dispensationalism later became a characteristic trait of fundamentalism. Many of the early fundamentalist authors used it as a convenient interpretive framework for sorting out the relationship between the Old and the New Testament.

According to dispensational theology, history is divided into a number of discrete periods, called dispensations. (The precise number varies from author to author, but seven is probably the most common number cited.) During each dispensation God governs mankind according to specific principles which define human responsibility toward God and other people. Since the various dispensations are completely distinct from each other, the rules by which God chose to deal with the people in one dispensation cannot be taken directly over into another dispensation and utilized. For example, since the Old Testament was written to the Jews, its teachings cannot be applied directly to the Christian church. Whenever God's plan for the Jews and God's plan for his church are confused, it becomes impossible to understand Scripture correctly.

The church throughout history has normally applied the Old Testament prophecies regarding Israel's millennial kingdom to the church; but in order to do that, it has had to interpret those prophecies allegorically or typologically. Darby countered that the Bible must be interpreted literally and that the Old Testament prophecies mean just exactly what they say. The church, as he saw it, is best understood as an interlude in God's work with the Jews. If some of the Old Testament prophecies remain unfulfilled—and some surely do—then that fact necessitates their future fulfillment. In particular, this means that God will someday intervene in history in order to establish an earthly millennial kingdom for the Jews. Dispensationalists are therefore staunchly premillennial (see p. 143).

Darby's system included several refinements on the basic premillennial position—for example, the pretribulational rapture of the church—but those details need not detain us here. What is important is the fact that his dispensational theology became extremely popular in the United States toward the end of the nineteenth century. Dwight L. Moody accepted many of his ideas. And shortly after the turn of the century, the dispensational system was embodied in an annotated edition of the King James Version, known as the Scofield Reference Bible. This remains the most successful study Bible ever published. In the second decade of this century, the advocates of dispensationalism joined hands with those who held the Princeton view (see p. 143) of inerrancy to form one of the most important elements of the opposition to liberalism in the United States. That marriage was surprising, since the Princeton school was not even premillennial, much less dispensational. But everyone at that time recognized that conservative Christians had to overlook differences regarding nonessentials in order to defend the fundamentals of the faith.

Today, over fifty years later, dispensationalism remains the consensus position within fundamentalist circles; within liberal circles it is virtually unknown. As usual evangelicalism displays a good deal of diversity. Some evangelicals continue to maintain the distinctive dispensational approach to eschatology. Others hold premillennial views, but have dropped Darby's theological framework. Still other evangelicals affirm postmillennialism or maintain the church's more traditional amillennial position.

The Evangelical Stance

Evangelicals in America have family ties which unite them with Christians in every age and in every part of the world. They have roots in the early church and medieval Catholicism. But there are three specific points in the history of the church which are particularly important for understanding this modern movement.

Evangelicals stand solidly with the Protestant Reformers. They hold to the unique authority of the Bible against those who bestow undue authority on tradition, reason or conscience. They teach the good news that God offers salvation freely to those who turn from sin and accept forgiveness through Jesus Christ. They teach that every Christian is called to a life of service and forgiveness.

At the beginning of the nineteenth century, evangelicalism was becoming the dominant form of Protestantism in the United States. Denominations and voluntary societies proliferated. On the frontier, the more formal, liturgical expressions of Protestant Christianity gave way to a more informal style appropriate to the environment. The vibrant energy of the period spilled over into a great outpouring of missionaries.

After the middle of the nineteenth century, American evangelicalism was forced to take a defensive stance against German higher criticism and Darwinian evolution. Conservatives began to call themselves fundamentalists and took their stand publicly against the liberal position. They insisted that it was unacceptable to dilute the core of the gospel to make it more compatible with the anti-Christian spirit of the age. God intervened in our history to bring us salvation in Jesus Christ. Furthermore, they said that those who have experienced salvation must not neglect the proclamation of that message in order to devote themselves solely to social concerns. The church must not in any way compromise the authority of Scripture, the integrity of the gospel or the missionary task.

Today, evangelicalism is re-emerging as the mainstream of American Protestantism. The adamant and unyielding repudiation by fundamentalists of the liberal attempt to dilute the gospel was an unpleasant, but necessary episode in the history of American evangelicalism. It is equally hard, but necessary for contemporary evangelicalism to disengage itself from the excesses of fundamentalism. Reverence for the Bible as God's inspired Word must not preclude careful scholarly study which utilizes the best critical tools. The gospel should neither become legalistic nor should it be diluted. Finally, the evangelical church must no longer tolerate the spirit of defensiveness and withdrawal. The church should be an open community in which committed men and women are used by God in his service. Contemporary evangelicals are learning again how to proclaim the message of God's redemptive love to all sectors of society.

Further Reading

Clouse, Robert G. *The Meaning of the Millennium.* Downers Grove, Ill.: InterVarsity Press, 1977. Essays by proponents of the four major views on the millennium.

Hamilton, Michael P., ed. *The Charismatic Movement.* Grand Rapids: Eerdmans, 1975. An excellent collection of essays which examines the movement from the perspective of both advocates and opponents.

Hummel, Charles E. *Fire in the Fireplace.* Downers Grove, Ill.: InterVarsity Press, 1978. A careful survey of the biblical and historical background of the charismatic movement.

Lindsell, Harold. *The Battle for the Bible.* Grand Rapids: Zondervan, 1976. An impassioned plea for the doctrine of "inerrancy."

Rogers, Jack, ed. *Biblical Authority.* Waco, Tex.: Word, 1977. A collection of essays on the inspiration and authority of the Bible. Written as a response to the book by Lindsell.

Thurman, L. Duane. *How to Think about Evolution.* Downers Grove, Ill.: InterVarsity Press, 1978. A balanced, objective approach to the controversy which analyzes the arguments on both sides and leaves readers to make up their own minds.

DYNAMICS
OF THE
CHRISTIAN LIFE

PART III

GROWING UP
IN CHRIST:
THE BASICS
OF SPIRITUAL LIFE

11

The distinctive quality of religious life among contemporary evangelicals stems from the historical traditions described in the last few chapters. The impact of the Reformation, the Puritan tradition, pietism, the frontier revivals and the fundamentalist-modernist controversy can all be felt in the styles of worship and assumptions about Christian growth. What exactly is the nature of religious life within evangelicalism? What are its distinctive emphases which set it apart from other forms of Christianity? What values unite contemporary evangelicals into one family? How can we recognize other members of the family when we meet them?

Evangelicals have always been convinced that if we open our lives in faith to Jesus Christ, we will be *personally* changed. After entering into a saving relationship with God's Son, we are to become progressively more like Christ. That transformation is one of the primary goals of salvation. The Scriptures teach that the

Holy Spirit works in us to effect change. Yet the New Testament also commands Christians to press on toward Christlikeness (Phil. 3:12). All of us, as Christians, are to strive to grow in spiritual maturity because growth does not happen automatically.

Daily Disciplines

Growing in Christ is not primarily a mystical or a psychological experience, although both elements are often present. It is a gradual process by which Christians grow toward holiness. In theology, this process of growth is referred to as *sanctification*. Prayer and Bible study are essential to the process. Only through God can one become holy, but God has chosen to use his Word and our communion with him in prayer as a means to that end. By communicating with God and reading his Word, we provide a way for the Holy Spirit to work in our lives.

What is prayer? It is talking to God. It is telling him of our feelings, our needs, our wants, our hopes. Prayer is the way we open our lives to God. Over and over, the New Testament instructs us to present our needs to God in faith. When we trust God, open our lives to his work and bring our cares to him, we obey Christ's command to pray in faith.

God knows our needs. He knows our helplessness. He knows that there is no area of our lives in which we are truly in control of our own destinies. Recognizing our own helplessness and dependency upon God, we are drawn to prayer.

God has linked his power to our prayers. He promises us forgiveness if we confess our sins. He invites us to make requests—for our own needs, for the needs of others, for the work of the church. In short, God invites us to open every aspect of our lives to his creative power.

Prayer is not just petition. It is the most direct expression of our relationship with God. It is often an act of worship. It is always an intimate dialog. As we open ourselves to God in prayer, he gives himself to us. He does not remain aloof. God comforts our anxieties, speaks to us of sin, draws us to confession and teaches us how to praise him. Prayer can be the most intense joy of our Christian lives. It is our communion with our Lord.

Sometimes, though, we may experience periods of dryness during which prayer is not a *joy* at all. Sometimes it is just plain work—and hard work at that. So one of the most important things to be said about prayer is that it is not merely an option in the Christian life. God has commanded us to pray (Phil. 4:6-7).

But if God's commands are just and good, why has he instructed us to devote ourselves to a task that is not always pleasant? There are many reasons. Prayer forces us to face and acknowledge our helplessness. We have to recognize our need in order to be healed. Moreover, prayer invites God to involve himself in our lives. He wants to help us to grow to be more like him, yet he waits for our invitation. He allows us to limit his creative power. That power is released in prayer.

Bible study. We talk to God in prayer. God speaks to us through his Word. As Paul wrote in his letter to the Romans, faith is awakened in us by hearing the message of Jesus Christ. Christians have always recognized that regular feeding on and responding to the Word nourishes Christian growth. God uses the words of the Bible both to kindle and to renew our faith. Through the Bible we learn how to become more Christlike. The Bible is the Christian's most important tool for living a moral life which will be pleasing to God. In part one we discussed how to interpret the Bible. But proper interpretation is worth little unless it is accompanied by obedience. Today, as yesterday, the strength of evangelical Christians lies in their knowledge of and submission to the living Word of God.

Devotions. As a practical outgrowth of this perspective, many evangelicals set aside a part of each day for "daily devotions" or "quiet time." Some people allow a few minutes in the morning before work; others take up to an hour or more. The goal, whether the time spent is brief or extended, is to insure that both prayer and Bible study are a regular part of one's life.

The rationale for the practice is excellent. If prayer and Bible study are important for nurturing spiritual growth, then it makes sense to regularize them. Many great Christians of the past followed this practice and recommended it to others.

Daily devotions, however, are not an obligation or a law which must be obeyed. To consider them so would be to confuse the means to the goal with the goal itself. The core value in the evangelical perspective on life is submission to the will of God. God has commanded us to pray and to study the Bible as a means toward that end. Private devotions, therefore, are one way—albeit a very effective way—of including those two disciplines in our lives.

Becoming like Christ

Man was created by God in his own image. When man fell into sin, that image was warped or marred; a tendency toward evil and destruction was introduced into all humanity. Consequently, we cannot trust our spontaneous inclinations for they are too often directed toward hurting others or exhalting ourselves. Our perception of what is right is so distorted that even when we honestly pursue it, we often fail.

God understands our plight, however, and that is why he has given us the Scriptures. God's Holy Spirit uses our prayerful study of the Bible as a means for renewing the image of God within us. Even though we are no longer chained by sin, sin remains an active force in the life of every Christian. Consequently, the Scriptures remain essential as a guide to how God wants us to live.

The Bible has sometimes been characterized as a book of "thou shalt not's" and Yahweh as a God of prohibitions. In a sense both are true. God knows that certain kinds of behavior destroy the very texture of what is truly human. But the goal of the law is not negative in the sense of being life quenching. Rather, God wants to protect us while we learn holiness and teach us how to love. Toward that end he has given us both his Word with its commands and its prohibitions and his Holy Spirit to apply the Word to each of us. If we respond to the Holy Spirit and trust God, that Word serves as a map to guide us back to our true humanity.

Evangelicals study the Bible in order to understand the history of God's work and to see the divine pattern for a truly liberated human existence. The Christian life is to be a life liberated from sin and in harmony with God. As we respond to the subtle work of the Holy Spirit, we learn to love as God has commanded. "We love, because he first loved us" (1 Jn. 4:19). That is the essential expression of Christianity. True freedom is living fully and completely to the glory of God by living within the limits defined by a biblical ethic. Only within those limits can we love our neighbors as God intended.

Antinomianism and legalism. Christians can, however, lose the freedom that God intended for us by falling into either of two extremes: antinomianism or legalism. Antinomian Christians believe that their faith in Christ frees them from any obligation to pursue holiness as defined by God's Word. An antinomian is a lawless person who loses his freedom through excess. Legalists, on the other hand, restrict their lives more narrowly than God intended. Legalism eliminates freedom by augmenting God's law with a manmade code designed to cover every contingency. Legalism forgets the spirit of the law (to help us to love our neighbors) and substitutes the letter of the law.

Antinomianism has cropped up occasionally throughout the history of Christianity, so the church must remain alert to its danger. But it has not been characteristic of evangelicalism. The strong biblical orientation within the evangelical community has acted as a protection against that particular problem. Legalism, however, has sometimes been a problem for us.

Ethical guidance within American evangelicalism has frequently been characterized by a strong orientation toward rules. One still hears, for example, that good Christians do not attend movies or smoke cigarettes. While this may be good advice, it cannot be considered a test of one's commitment. A truly Christian ethic allows for a degree of freedom. Biblical freedom is always freedom to love God and serve one's neighbor. Hence a rule-book approach which reduces Christian ethics to refraining from a limited set of behaviors (many of which are not even mentioned in the Bible) is clearly wrong-headed.

The will of God. Evangelicals frequently talk about *finding the will of God.* The concept plays a very important role in evangelical piety and ethics because it communicates the importance of being completely committed to becoming what God intends us to be. Evangelical Christians have always been convinced that commitment to God must be total.

The phrase *finding the will of God* is biblical to the extent that it communicates the importance of a full commitment to him. But the phrase has come to communicate the idea that God has an *individual* plan for each person and that any person who finds the plan and lives in obedience to it will experience God's blessing. While this plan may not be explicitly revealed in the Bible, it is always within its precepts. Each of us is responsible to find the plan and live by it. This secondary use of the phrase has little biblical basis and has caused young Christians tremendous anxiety.

Finding God's will is not a mysterious, mystical experience. God gave us his Word and his Spirit to help us apply that Word in our own lives. As we read the Word, we grow in our understanding of the character of God. We learn about Jesus Christ, God's self-revelation, in the pages of the Gospels. We hear Paul's exhortations to holiness. But our growing understanding does not automatically make us Christlike. There is also an element of will, of submission to the sanctifying work of the Holy Spirit. To find the will of God is to understand the biblical perspective, to grasp what it means to be Christlike, and to obey in each particular.

These brief discussions of prayer, Bible study and ethics are simply condensations of what most evangelicals believe. The treatments are short and descriptive because you are not meant to stop here. Many good books have been written on these topics. I encourage you to explore the available evangelical literature and to read about these topics in depth. I have only tried to whet your appetite.

Further Reading

Barclay, Oliver R. *Guidance.* Downers Grove, Ill.: InterVarsity Press, 1978. A short examination of the biblical material on guidance.

Crotts, Stephen M. *If You Haven't Got a Prayer.* Downers Grove, Ill.: Inter-Varsity Press, 1978. A light, readable beginner's guide to prayer.

Hallesby, O. *Prayer.* Minneapolis: Augsburg Pub. House, 1931. Excellent reflections on various aspects of individual, private prayer.

Houghton, Frank, ed. *The Quiet Time.* Downers Grove, Ill.: InterVarsity Press, 1976. A brief, practical pamphlet on the place of a quiet time in the life of a serious Christian.

White, John. *The Fight.* Downers Grove, Ill.: InterVarsity Press, 1976. A personal look at the basic areas of the Christian life—prayer, Bible study, evangelism, faith, fellowship, work and guidance.

See the bibliography following chapters two through five for works related to the study of the Bible.

REACHING OUT
IN CHRIST: MINISTRY
TO OTHERS

12

When we accept the gift of salvation offered by Jesus Christ, we not only receive a new relationship with God, we also become members of the body of Christ. Just as life in relationship with God is both a gift and a task, so living in relationship with God's people is both a joy and a duty. We were commanded by Jesus Christ to "love one another." That love is to extend not only to other Christians, but also to non-Christians the world over. Because of their commitment to live in obedience to their Lord, evangelicals accept a share in the mission of the church.

The Invisible Body
When I speak of the church as a spiritual family, I am not merely speaking affectionately. The truth is far deeper than that. The spiritual links which bind all Christians together as a family are every bit as real as (and often stronger than) the links which created a natural family. God himself ordained that complex set

of relationships to be the context in which Christians grow toward full spiritual maturity.

Ministry. The totality of all Christians throughout the whole world and throughout all time has traditionally been called the "invisible church." Mutual ministry, that is, serving and being served, is supposed to be characteristic of the relationships among members of the church. Usually we use the term *minister* to refer to a particular person in the church who fulfills certain special tasks. But our language leads us astray. The Bible teaches very clearly that God has called every member of the body of Christ, the church, to be a minister of the gospel (Eph. 4:1-17).

The church has always recognized that God enables some people to minister to the spiritual needs of those around them with unusual effectiveness. These people have therefore been set apart and supported by the rest of the Christian community so that they can devote all of their time to ministry. Some of these people have been evangelists, some teachers and some counselors. But the fact that the church calls "ministers" to devote their full time to the task should not lead us to the mistaken conclusion that the rest of us need not minister at all.

It is impossible for one or two people to minister to a whole congregation. God did not intend one person to carry that kind of burden. The burdens of ministry must be shared. When all Christians recognize that they are called to nurture each other in fellowship and love, the church grows stronger. God intends every member of every church to be a minister to others.

We are all called to exert ouselves to the fullest possible extent in order to help our brothers and sisters in Christ grow toward wholeness. Likewise, our Christian brothers and sisters are called by Christ to minister to us. Christ said that God's law for us can be summed up in two commandments: "Love the Lord your God with all your heart, and with all your soul, and with all your mind. . . . Love your neighbor as yourself" (Mt. 22:37, 39). Whenever love for our neighbors leads us to do something which aids their growth, whenever love leads us to comfort a person in any way, we are ministering. Sometimes ministry is directed toward physical well-being, other times toward spiritual growth. The distinction must not obscure the fact that ministry is the act of caring for people in need. And God's true church is a network of ministers under the leadership of Jesus Christ.

The gifts of the Spirit. In 1 Corinthians 12, Paul begins by reminding readers that God gives Christians gifts or abilities which enable them to serve the church. Some Christians, for example, are gifted by God to be evangelists; others are given the ability to comprehend the Scriptures; others receive the ability to heal. Like the diverse organs in a human body, each Christian has a particular function in the body of Christ. This diversity of gifts is essential to the life of the church. Without it, the church could neither sustain itself nor serve society, just as a physical body could not survive with two hearts and no lungs. Diversity in the church expresses a fundamental unity which exists under the headship of Christ. All the parts work together to do God's will.

In 1 Corinthians 12, Paul makes several other points worth noting. First of all, every Christian receives the gift of God's choice. Christians need not be ashamed of their place in the body since it is God who put them there. Each person has something to contribute to the fellowship.

Second, every person who has been given a gift by God is essential to the function of the church. Each of us has real value and worth. By faith we must accept that truth about ourselves and our fellow Christians. We are called by Christ to give up our independence and to recognize our mutual reliance on each other.

Third, there is no single gift that is essential to a fully developed Christian life. No one need feel embarrassed or inadequate because there is a gift he or she does not have. Rather, we should praise God for what we have and use it for the nurturing of the body.

Finally, the *gifts* of the Spirit *to us* must not be confused with the *fruit* of the Spirit *within us.* We are given gifts of the Spirit so that we can more effectively serve one another. But if we become preoccupied with the gifts by which we serve, and thus neglect *the people* we are called to love, we pervert the work the Spirit has given us. The fruit of the Spirit are "love, joy, peace, patience, kindness, goodness, faithfulness, gentleness, self-control" (Gal. 5:22-23). These are the marks of a mature Christian. Without these fruits, our spiritual gifts are nothing—they are of no use to us or to the fellowship of Christians (1 Cor. 13:1-3).

The Visible Body
The universal church consists of the fellowship of all believers all over the world. This concept is, of course, a theoretical one. In our fallen world we try to approximate this fellowship in our local, denominational churches. In the last decade or so, the image of the visible, local church has become somewhat tarnished, even to those who subscribe to the theoretical discussion regarding the invisible, universal church. This situation, along with the American tendency toward individualism, has led some evangelicals to drop out of the institutional church altogether. Why be part of a local congregation where some people are hypocritical, where a lot of time seems wasted on fruitless meetings and where mediocrity seems to be the norm?

Acts 2:42 records that the first Christians met together for four reasons: instruction, fellowship, breaking of bread and prayer. This particular verse does not set out those four purposes as a norm. It merely describes the practice of the early church. But in the light of the whole New Testament it is clear that those four activities accurately reflect the most basic concerns of the first Christians.

It is possible for Christians to worship God individually (that is, in isolation) but the early church recognized the inadequacy of that approach. It is not consistent with the nature of the Christian faith.

The fact that Jews and Gentiles worshiped together in the early church manifested the power of God and his work in and through his people. Today, the situation is similar. As new believers from diverse backgrounds confess their faith in Christ and enter the fellowship, the body receives encouragement. Singing praises to God together helps to unite the membership. And Christ himself is present in a special way wherever his people meet in his name.

Second, it is in the context of corporate worship that Christians gradually learn a new perspective on life. They are taught the basic doctrines of the church and the meaning of symbols, such as baptism and the bread and the wine which are used in worship. Biblical ethical standards and values for living will gradually be made clear. Because the ministry of teaching is one of the gifts of the Spirit given to the Christian community, it is in the church that one should learn the teachings of the apostles and the implications of those concepts for the Christian life. The church as a corporate body plays an essential role in the learning process.

Third, the church provides an appropriate context for prayer. The most pressing needs of the community are to be lifted up to God in public prayer as part of the worship service. In addition, many Christians meet together in smaller groups to share more private needs and to pray for each other. The church as a corporate body nurtures individual members through this ministry of prayer, and new Christians have the privilege of becoming a part of this circle of interdependency.

Finally, the church is a place of fellowship or koinonia. Because the word *fellowship* has been used of fairly casual social relationships, some Christians have chosen to use the Greek word koinonia to refer to the relationship which Christians share because Christ has brought them together by his Spirit. The word emphasizes the unusually deep level of communication and concern which has been made possible for those of us who have experienced the love of God in Jesus Christ. As John said, "We love, because he first loved us." Koinonia speaks of a commitment to caring and sharing which partakes of the power of God. It speaks of a commitment to bear each other's burdens which goes beyond mere friendship.

A Christian is not merely one who is reconciled with God as

an individual or who is reconciled with other Christians on a one-to-one basis, though both are true. A Christian is one who has been called by God into God's community. Only within the context of a Christian community where worship, instruction, prayer and fellowship occur can one grow into full Christian maturity. The visible church is the community of redeemed people. It is God's vehicle for bringing men and women to personal and corporate wholeness, to the full expression of their life in Christ.

If you were to visit a variety of local congregations, you would find the four elements of worship discussed in the previous section. But the way in which local congregations strive to implement those four elements will vary widely. All churches, for example, recognize the importance of prayer. But one church will have a prayer meeting each Wednesday night while another will have a network of small prayer groups meeting at various times and places. Since the Scriptures neither command nor sanction any particular format, this variety is legitimate and to be expected.

There are, however, other differences within the evangelical community which are taken more seriously. While these differences are not actually divisive, evangelical congregations tend to defend their own approach with vigor. To be specific, evangelicals often disagree among themselves about the proper relationship between the local congregation and those called into the ministry, about the proper form of church government and about the correct form for public worship.

New Christians will need to recognize that there is some biblical support for each of these various points of view. At the same time none of them can be conclusively proven. Yet ideally these differences regarding the structure and function of the local church should never be allowed to obscure the more central areas where there is substantial agreement.

Most Protestant congregations in the United States are organized into denominational groups. Members of a local church are indirectly members of a denomination. The distinctions between the denominations are based on doctrinal disagreements with the long histories described in earlier chapters. Baptists, for example, insist that only believers should be baptized, while Lutherans baptize the children of believing parents. Other American denominations came about as a result of immigration patterns among the early settlers, and still others resulted from historical events such as the Civil War (see chapter nine).

This division between believers is very unfortunate. It is not what God intended, but we must try to work with the situation as best we can. Christians must involve themselves in Christian communities where they can experience koinonia, be encouraged toward Christian maturity, and enter fully into the life of the church. Prayer and Bible study are essential for Christian growth, but by themselves they will be ineffective. Christian fellowship is also essential. The church is the chosen instrument of God to carry out the work of reconciliation begun by Jesus Christ. We would be both foolish and disobedient to refuse to participate in the life of the Christian community.

How the Body Reaches Out
God has ordained that the universal church will not die. But a local congregation, like all other organisms, may either grow or die out. When Christians in a local church take the attitude that outreach is unnecessary and turn their sights inward, that congregation begins to die. Fortunately the converse is also true. When a local congregation intentionally devotes its energy to reaching beyond its boundaries, that body of believers grows.

The church has been called upon to reach beyond itself for two reasons: to take the gospel to those who have not yet heard the message, and to stand for justice, unity and healing in a world full of injustice, pain and suffering.

The church reaching out with the Christian message. Why should the church propagate the gospel? Evangelism seems to imply that Christianity is the only true religion. Is this the case? Evangelicals respond with a unanimous yes. This is one of the places where the evangelical perspective on the Christian faith differs most clearly from more liberal perspectives. There have been many great religious thinkers throughout history who have taught people how to live with regard to spiritual things. If Jesus were merely a great teacher, on a par with other great teachers, then evangelism would be unnecessary. But evangelicals hold that Jesus is more than the greatest of religious teachers. He is rather the culmination of God's revelation. Jesus is the incarnation of almighty God. He is Emmanuel, which means "God with us." When Jesus said, "I am the way, and the truth, and the life; no one comes to the Father, but by me," he claimed absolute uniqueness for himself (Jn. 14:6). He claimed that salvation was available only through himself.

If the Bible were merely the product of religious reflection, then the church's concern to propagate the gospel would indeed be out of place. But evangelicals have always insisted that God has revealed himself through the Old Testament, the New Testament and pre-eminently through Jesus Christ. Is the Christian message true? Yes. But that is not the primary point. The primary point is that the message is *God-given*. Herein lies the exclusive claim of Christianity.

This exclusive claim does not imply that there is no truth or value in other religions. But it implies that the greatest truths are found in a biblical faith. We read the Bible because God has promised to speak through his Word. We read other religious literature with the awareness that it may be profoundly moving and helpful, but that it is not the inspired Word of God. That is why Christians feel that it is a service to tell others about Christ. But in the end this is not the central issue. The central issue is that God commanded us to proclaim to all people the message of his love and forgiveness available through Christ's unique sacrifice. Evangelical Christians are committed to obeying that command.

Personal evangelism. Before he ascended into heaven, Jesus promised his followers that he would send them the Holy Spirit who would give them power to be witnesses for Christ. On the day of Pentecost the Holy Spirit came upon the disciples and

Peter was moved to proclaim the gospel to the crowds that gathered. Shortly afterward the religious authorities in Jerusalem ordered the disciples to refrain from preaching about Jesus. Of course, they refused to comply. In time the opposition boiled over into active persecution which drove many of the early Christians out of Jerusalem. Yet we read in the book of Acts that they continued to share the news about the death and resurrection of Jesus Christ.

This process of sharing your faith with others is called evangelism. It can be done publicly before large groups or privately with a close friend or neighbor. But it must be done because God has commanded it. We should also consider it a privilege to let others know about the faith which gives meaning to our lives. Sometimes a friend or neighbor will reject our faith. But at other times they will joyfully accept the redemption that Christ has provided for them. Christians of all ages have discovered that the message of salvation speaks to the real needs of those around them.

Many people today—perhaps most—believe quite sincerely that the Christian faith is solely an ethical system. They try to live a moral life, most of the time. And they hope that their efforts will be considered adequate when they must come face to face with God. In short, many people have never really grasped the gospel message. In the light of that situation, committed Christians are called by God to look for opportunities to share their faith whenever possible. Evangelical Christians take the responsibility to evangelize seriously.

Missions. It is one thing to share the gospel with those you come in contact with every day. But we must also be concerned about people in other cultures and other countries who have never heard the gospel of salvation. It is widely recognized today that each culture has its religious forms. Furthermore, missionaries have in the past been responsible for cultural disintegration in various parts of the world. So critics demand that the church recognize the relativity of values and cultural norms. They insist that it is time to admit that Christianity is a part of the

Western cultural heritage and should not be exported to non-Western areas of the world.

Evangelicals are willing to acknowledge that much of this criticism is justified. Missionaries have often been cultural chauvinists and as a result have disrupted societies by forcing Western standards on them. But evangelicals insist that the solution is not withdrawal, but better training. Missionaries must be taught to distinguish between their own cultural heritage and the gospel of God's love and forgiveness.

Having done that, evangelicals will continue to send missionaries who will be disruptive, for the gospel itself is inherently disruptive. It challenges cultural norms in all areas of the world. That is what it is supposed to do. Jesus warned that his message would sometimes cause division. So we cannot take disrupted lives as a sign that mission work has gone wrong. It may, in fact, be a sign of success. Some of the turmoil may be the work of the Spirit. In the end, evangelicals will not be able to offer an answer which will satisfy their critics. Nonetheless, they will continue to proclaim the gospel of Jesus Christ to all people. Evangelicals cannot acknowledge that all religions are equally satisfactory. They cannot affirm religious relativism.

The church reaching out in compassion. Both Israel and the church were elected by God for a task. Both were called to proclaim his moral demands and his promise of love, forgiveness and reconciliation. Likewise, the people of God have been commanded to translate their religious commitments into concrete action.

Although the Old Testament prophets sometimes talked about the future, more often they proclaimed God's judgment upon evil in their own society. They insisted that God would totally and unconditionally reject the religious offerings of the people when they were presented within an unjust society.

By Jesus' time the political situation was entirely different. Israel was no longer free but under the rule of Rome. Yet Jesus' demand for social justice is essentially the same as that of the prophets before him. At a very early point in his ministry Jesus visited the synagogue in Nazareth. There he was asked to read the Scripture lesson for the day (Is. 61:1-2), which stated that God would send someone to "preach good news to the poor. . . . proclaim release to the captives and recovering of sight to the blind, to set at liberty those who are oppressed" (Lk. 4:18). It was a text with radical social implications. After he had finished reading, Jesus announced that Isaiah's message had been fulfilled on that day. Social concern was a core element in Jesus' proclamation of the kingdom of God.

The early church, by taking concrete steps to see that widows were cared for (Acts 6), continued the pattern of social concern. Paul once took time away from his active missionary ministry to travel to Jerusalem with aid for the Christians who were suffering under a severe famine. In the book of James we learn that true religion is "to visit orphans and widows in their affliction, and to keep oneself unstained from the world" (Jas. 1:27). Later in the same book James denounces the rich who attain their wealth by underpaying their workers. In sum, the social implications of the good news were not peripheral. Both the Old and New Testaments teach that true faith leads to individual holiness *and* social concern.

Throughout its history the church has demonstrated a clear understanding of her responsibility to be compassionate toward those in need. During the so-called Dark Ages it was the church that carried on the task of education. During the feudal period, a period which bordered on anarchy, the church was active in the peace movement. During the Reformation, Luther, Zwingli and Calvin worked with their respective governments to produce a more just society. Zwingli, for example, was responsible for opening a poorhouse in Zurich which served soup and bread each morning to the needy. In the eighteenth century, England was awakened to its responsibilities toward the poor and defenseless as a result of the work of John Wesley and the evangelical revival. William Wilberforce, an English evangelical of that period, led the fight in the English Parliament against the slave traffic. Some fifty years later, Lord Shaftesbury, another Eng-

lishman, fought for more humane working conditions for laborers in the factories. During the same period in the United States
some evangelicals were actively involved in the abolitionist
movement. And during the chaos of the Civil War they worked
to bring both the gospel and medical care to soldiers.

But toward the end of the nineteenth century, all of this
changed. Conservative evangelicals in the United States began
to withdraw their support from efforts designed to bring society
at large closer to the Christian ideal. Since that time two generations of American conservative evangelicals have been taught
to believe that they must choose between the gospel of personal
salvation and concern for justice and righteousness in society.
Thus, during the height of the civil-rights movement in the
1960s, a movement which was spearheaded by a Baptist minister
(Martin Luther King, Jr.) and the Southern Christian Leadership Conference, most evangelicals were silent. This is changing
today.

Contemporary American evangelicals are beginning to see
again that the split between social concern and evangelism is a
recent aberration. It is not, most emphatically, the normal state
of affairs in the church. Many people have publicly acknowledged this mistake and are taking concrete steps to do something about it. The movement for change is very recent, so there
is still much to criticize. But the atmosphere has changed. The
threat of liberalism no longer blinds evangelicals to the biblical
mandate to implement the gospel for the good of society.

The Family Heritage

Well, that's the family. I warned you at the beginning that some
of our family feuds have been pretty fierce, and we have always
had our share of eccentrics. But at the same time, it is a great
family. The dialog and the fellowship which the Holy Spirit
creates within it are, at times, unexcelled.

The family resemblance should have become clear in your
mind by now. If you see it clearly, you will have little trouble
recognizing the members of the clan.

Evangelical Christians are, first of all, serious about trying to understand Scripture. If you attend a church where the Scriptures are taught, that church is in all probability evangelical. If the people there are interested in grasping the intent of the original authors, they are probably evangelical. Evangelicals sometimes disagree about how to interpret the Bible, about which translation to use or about how to define terms like *inspiration*. But people only argue about things they think are important. And evangelicals agree on the importance of this basic premise: The Bible is God's authoritative and inspired Word to us and as such, it deserves our serious efforts to understand and respond to it. Evangelicals accept that call. That is one of the ways you can recognize a member of the family. He or she will value God's Word.

Second, evangelicals consistently proclaim the good news about Jesus Christ. They agree that men and women are blinded by sin and can do nothing about their situation. They believe that each person needs to be reconciled with God and that Jesus Christ lived and died to destroy the power of sin and to create a way back to God. Evangelicals want everyone to know that he or she can be reconciled with God by turning to him through faith in Jesus Christ. Christians are so convinced of this good news that they continually invent new ways to communicate the message. They recognize that the very message can be offensive in that it speaks of human sin and need. Nonetheless, they are willing to risk that rather than deny another person the opportunity to hear of God's love.

Finally, evangelical Christians persistently seek to become like Jesus Christ. For them the Christian life consists not merely in assent to a doctrinal statement, a commitment to attend church on Sunday or a desire to establish casual social relationships with other Christians. They are committed to a personal relationship with Jesus Christ which leads them to try to become like him. As a means to that end Christians seek deep fellowship with other believers which includes prayer, Bible study and worship. Sure, there is disagreement on what kind of lifestyle most adequately reflects the gospel. Yet evangelical Christians are agreed that God's love will transform a person's character over a period of time. Evangelical Christians anticipate their own growth in holiness with pleasure. They trust the Holy Spirit to bring the work of salvation to completion within themselves and their brethren.

The evangelical family is lively. It is constantly bursting into new life in some out-of-the-way place. And the most unexpected individuals are frequently brought into the family. The Holy Spirit is, of course, at work in other branches of the Christian faith. Evangelicals recognize that fact, but hold that these important elements must be present in order to express Christianity in its fullness.

How does all of this affect us personally? Well, it gives us clues about how to recognize relatives in the faith. When we meet someone who recognizes the power and authority of God's Word, who revels in the fact that God's love was so great that he sent his Son to die for us, and who daily grows in maturity in Christ—when we meet someone like that, we have met a member of the family!

Further Reading

Anderson, J. N. D. *Christianity and Comparative Religion.* Downers Grove, Ill.: InterVarsity Press, 1970. A brief but stimulating discussion of the uniqueness of Christianity and the implications of that fact for the way Christians view other religions and for understanding the task of missions.

Blauw, Johannes. *The Missionary Nature of the Church: A Survey of the Biblical Theology of Mission.* Grand Rapids: Eerdmans, 1962. Beginning with the book of Genesis, the author shows that Christian missions are an essential expression of biblical faith.

Goldsmith, Martin. *Don't Just Stand There!* Downers Grove, Ill.: InterVarsity Press, 1976. A first book on God's world mission, summarizing biblical teaching and what we can do.

Hatfield, Mark. *Between a Rock and a Hard Place.* Waco, Tex.: Word, 1976. The evangelical senator from Oregon discusses the place of evangelicals in politics.

Little, Paul E. *How to Give Away Your Faith.* Downers Grove, Ill.: InterVarsity Press, 1966. A practical and sensitive approach to communicating the gospel.

Mains, Karen B. *Open Heart-Open Home.* Elgin, Ill.: David C. Cook, 1976.

Moberg, David O. *The Great Reversal: Evangelism versus Social Concern.* Philadelphia: Lippincott, 1972. An examination of recent evangelical negligence regarding the social implications of the gospel.

Perkins, John. *A Quiet Revolution.* Waco, Tex.: Word, 1976. A proposal for wholistic ministry including economic development, social action, evangelism and justice, formulated out of the author's experiences in working in Mississippi.

Snyder, Howard A. *The Problem of Wineskins: Church Structure in a Technological Age.* Downers Grove, Ill.: InterVarsity Press, 1975. A provocative biblical study of church structure and its relationship to the church's effectiveness in modern society.

Stedman, Ray C. *Body Life.* Glendale, Calif.: Regal, 1972. A solidly biblical exposition of the way the body of Christ should function.

Stott, John R. W. *Christian Mission in the Modern World.* Downers Grove, Ill.: InterVarsity Press, 1975. An examination of the church's role in evangelism, discipleship and social action throughout the world.

Index